DØØ61310

Contents

The
Market
Research
Toolbox

SECOND EDITION

The
Market
Research
Toolbox

A Concise Guide
for Beginners

SECOND EDITION

Edward F. McQuarrie

Santa Clara University

SAGE Publications
Thousand Oaks ▪ London ▪ New Delhi

For information:

Sage Publications, Inc.
2455 Teller Road
Thousand Oaks, California 91320
E-mail: order@sagepub.com

Sage Publications Ltd.
1 Oliver's Yard
55 City Road
London EC1Y 1SP
United Kingdom

Sage Publications India Pvt. Ltd.
B-42, Panchsheel Enclave
Post Box 4109
New Delhi 110 017 India

Printed in the United States of America

Library of Congress Cataloging-in-Publication Data

McQuarrie, Edward F.
The market research toolbox: A concise guide for beginners /
Edward F. McQuarrie. — 2nd ed.
        p. cm.
Includes bibliographical references and index.
ISBN 1-4129-1318-7 (cloth) — ISBN 1-4129-1319-5 (pbk.)
    1. Marketing research—Methodology. I. Title.
HF5415.2.M383 2006
658.8′3—dc22   2005006695

This book is printed on acid-free paper.

    06   07   08   09   8   7   6   5   4   3   2

Acquisitions Editor:	Al Bruckner
Editorial Assistant:	MaryAnn Vail
Production Editor:	Diane S. Foster
Copy Editor:	David Kaplan
Typesetter:	C&M Digitals, (P) Ltd.
Proofreader:	Scott Oney
Indexer:	Molly Hall
Cover Designer:	Janet Foulger

Preface

M arket research refers to any effort to gather information about markets or customers. Market research is more necessary today than ever before because of the increased complexity of the business environment. At the level of specific industries or firms, whenever there is increased uncertainty the need for market research becomes more acute. That is, whenever markets change character, or economic conditions fluctuate, or competition intensifies, or technology evolves rapidly, the payoff from doing effective market research can be substantial.

Beginning in the 1980s, the kinds of firms that invest heavily in market research and the kinds of people who get involved in market research began to change. Prior to that point, mainstream packaged-goods companies were the major practitioners of market research, and the number of people who directly participated in market research was limited. Internal to the firm, the market research department was charged with hiring and supervising outside consultants on a project-by-project basis. These consulting firms in turn employed technical specialists in questionnaire design, statistical analysis, and so forth. The firm's marketing managers, in consultation with market research staff, set the basic parameters of the research study before it was put out to bid. Lastly, executives set overall budgets and chose whether to heed the results of the research. And that was that. Research and development (R&D) engineers did not materially participate, except to receive the final report. The quality function had scarcely been invented.

Today a much wider range of businesses feel the need to conduct market research, including manufacturers of high-technology products and providers of financial services. Similarly, a much more diverse group of employees has gotten involved in the design and conduct of market research. This is partly because some of the newer techniques cannot be delegated to specialists, and mostly because the contemporary business environment demands that *everyone* in the firm be customer- and market-focused. Three types of nonmarketing participants are worthy of special note: (1) engineers, including the design and development engineers who create new products, the manufacturing engineers who install and maintain production processes, and the technical services engineers and application specialists who do post-sales work with customers; (2) Quality professionals whose responsibilities now extend far beyond inspecting products for defects toward the achievement of total customer satisfaction; and (3) industrial designers, human interface specialists, and others who focus on the interaction between product and user. In most firms these people do not have a standard marketing or even business education. Nonetheless, the pressures of business require that they grasp the basic procedures for learning about customers and markets. Such learning has become a crucial part of their job responsibilities.

In light of the growing interest in and need for market research, this book was written to fill a gap. Although hundreds of books on market research have been published, most follow one of two models: (1) thick tomes surveying the whole subject of market research and intended for use as textbooks in university classrooms; and (2) thin volumes, covering one technique only, often at an advanced level, and aimed at an audience of specialists. What did not exist at the time of writing was a *thin* volume intended to provide an *overview* to the interested reader seeking a place to *begin*. The assumption underlying this book is that you need to get your bearings (What is conjoint analysis anyway?), to conduct some market research (Would a focus group make sense here?), or perhaps to interpret a market research effort that someone else has championed (Can I trust the results of this survey?).

In a second departure, this book is written primarily for *managers.* In tone, manner, and approach, the envisioned reader is a manager who has to decide whether or not to do market research, what objectives to pursue, and what specific kind of research to implement. This book is not a textbook as that term is generally understood. It does not conform to university pacing, style, tone, or degree of abstraction. Instead, the treatment strives to be concrete and specific: Do this. Don't do that. Watch out for this problem. Try this solution. The guiding idea is that managers are impatient people subject to conflicting demands who must act now. This book offers a practical approach addressed to their needs. Because of that orientation, this book is also suitable for use in a range of courses aimed at working professional students (e.g., part-time MBA students).

A third departure is a focus on business-to-business and technology examples. Modern market research as we know it was pioneered in the 1930s, 1940s, and 1950s to meet the needs of companies like Procter & Gamble, Quaker Oats, and Ralston Purina. Soap, cereal, pet food, and the like continue to be prominent among the examples and illustrations used to teach market research in the typical university course. This is entirely appropriate for textbooks aimed at a broad audience because consumer packaged-goods companies continue to spend large sums on market research and to provide many of the career opportunities in market research. However, living in California's Silicon Valley, my experience base is different. The research problems with which I am familiar preoccupy companies like Hewlett-Packard, Apple Computer, Cisco, and Sun Microsystems. Markets are small and concentrated, products are complex and expensive, customer expenditures are driven by the need to solve real business problems, and technologies are dynamic and rapidly changing. Although much of the accumulated wisdom of market research is just as relevant to Hewlett-Packard as to Procter & Gamble, it has to be taught differently. The readers I have in mind are impatient with examples based on the marketing of detergent to housewives. They don't want to have to make the translation from mass markets, simple products, and stable technologies to their own rather different situation.

If you fall within the core audience for this book, then you are a beginner and not a specialist. One of the important contributions of the book is to direct you to further reading. There exists an enormous amount of specialized material on market research. Part of my job is to help you sort through it so that you can find the next book that you need to read. If you intend to execute a particular market research project yourself, you certainly will need to read more than this book—for the sake of brevity, this book won't go into a great deal of depth on any single technique, but will merely open the toolbox and explain its contents and application. This book *will* tell you what a hammer is, what it does to a nail, when it is useful to drive nails, and when you might be better off using a bolt and wrench, but it won't train you to do carpentry. The assumption throughout is that "carpenters" (experts) are available to you. Thus, the focus can be on the background context and the questions that need to be asked *before* you hire a carpenter (or embark on your self-taught career as a carpenter).

Plan of the Book

Part I describes how to think about market research in the context of business decisions. Market research is only a *means to the end* of business success. It aids in but can never guarantee the achievement of profit. Market research almost always costs money—hard, assignable dollars that come out of an individual manager's budget. Therefore, like any investment, market research has to be justified in terms of an expected return. Part I answers questions about what market research is, what kinds of market research techniques exist, what objectives can be met by market research, and what payoff to expect from market research. The purpose of Part I is to equip you with the necessary vocabulary and organizing concepts to think intelligently about how market research might assist you in your own situation.

Part II describes six essential market research techniques: secondary research, customer visits, focus groups, surveys using questionnaires, conjoint analysis, and experimentation. These are the techniques that generally come to mind in business circles when one mentions market research. Each technique is discussed using a standard format: how it works, who does what when, examples or applications, cautionary notes, tips for success, and further reading.

Part II also includes chapters addressing two fundamental skills that underlie the effective use of most market research techniques. These skills involve (1) how to determine the number of customers to include in the research, along with procedures for identifying them; and (2) how to analyze the data produced via market research. The departure from the conventional textbook approach is most stark in the case of these two chapters. The typical market research textbook, whether undergraduate or graduate, devotes hundreds of pages to sampling theory and to the statistical analysis of data. The goal in this book is more limited: to provide the briefest possible introduction to these foundational skills consistent with providing useful insights for the managerial reader. The fact of the matter is that most managers outsource to specialists the tasks of drawing a sample and analyzing the data. Nonetheless, managers are responsible for selecting these specialists and vetting the results of their efforts. These two chapters aim to give a manager in that situation a leg up.

Part III of the book describes some typical applications of the standard market research techniques. The goal here is twofold: first, to link individual research techniques to the business problems for which they are best suited; and second, to show how multiple research techniques can be combined over time to address large-scale business problems. That is, execution of a single market research technique may be sufficient to answer some specific question or to close some narrowly defined knowledge gap. However, most substantial business challenges, such as selecting a new market to enter, or deciding where new product development efforts should be focused, require the application of multiple research techniques in sequence over time. Thus, Part III gives examples of how techniques can be combined and sequenced.

Who Should Read This Book?

Product Manager–Marketing. You may already have a business education, perhaps an MBA, and may even have one or more market research courses under your belt. If so, this book provides a refresher course, reinforcing your grasp of basic principles now that your schooling lies years in the past. Perhaps more important, it provides a resource that you can give to members of your work group, in order to bring them up to speed on the contribution of market research generally and the rationale for individual research techniques. Especially in technology firms, market research won't get done—or worse, won't get used—unless multiple constituencies, outside the product management function, accept the need for and value delivered by market research. Thus, this book can help to elevate the discussion of research issues in your workgroup. Finally, if you are in a business-to-business or technology firm, you may also find this book helpful in linking your business education, which probably emphasized packaged-goods examples, to your current job, with its rather different imperatives.

R&D Project Manager. You have the responsibility to create and design, with development of a new product the clearest example. It is your job to marshal people and resources to achieve a project goal. Today that includes doing market research. Although you can reasonably expect considerable assistance from marketing staff, the effectiveness of the market research done for you will often be a crucial determinant of the project's success; hence, there is a limit to how much you can delegate in this area. You will probably be among the most intent and focused readers of this book inasmuch as when you finish you will have to *act:* to request a budget, spend money, commit employee time. This book tries to answer as many of your questions as possible.

Program Manager. Your responsibilities are similar in many respects to those of the project manager, with one crucial exception: your output is seldom anything so tangible as a new product. Most of what you do consists of enhancing, improving, supplementing, or supporting your firm's central products or services (or maintaining and averting any decline in the quality of those products or services). In consequence, the budgets you directly control are typically minimal (if any even exist!). You will be particularly interested in those parts of this book that describe low-cost and no-cost approaches to gathering information on markets and customers.

Engineers. You're curious about the market research techniques you hear mentioned. You're probably also a little skeptical about whether market research is of any use in your particular situation, where technical innovation is key. This book will help you to make informed decisions about whether to embark upon or accept the results of particular market research efforts.

Quality Professional. Your charge today is customer satisfaction, not defect minimization. Depending on the culture of your firm, you may have assumed responsibilities classically assigned to the marketing function, that is, building a commitment to customer satisfaction on the part of employees throughout the firm. You have solid statistical training but have grown uneasy about the heavy reliance on surveys commonly found within the quality literature. This books helps you to grasp the possibilities inherent in the whole toolbox. It also helps you to think about statistics in the context of social science—that is, the behavior of humans—rather than the production context where your statistical education probably began.

Executive. You are at a level where business strategy is set. Like many contemporary executives, you are probably receptive to the idea that being market focused is important, but, also like many, you are not entirely sure how this laudable goal can be implemented in a timely and cost-effective manner. For you, this book serves two purposes. It provides a briefing and reminder of what market research can and cannot do (this is particularly helpful if your background is technical and not business-based), and it provides a resource that you can recommend to your people and to the training function within your firm.

Instructor. You may be considering this book for use in a market research course. For such courses, this book makes the most sense when any of the following hold true:

- The students are working professionals in an MBA or other master's program
- You intend to emphasize case analysis over data analysis
- The students are oriented more toward issues facing technology and business-to-business firms, rather than to those facing packaged-goods firms
- You find the standard textbook treatment of market research unsuitable to your purposes

Outside the context of a market research course, this book may be a useful supplement in courses on product planning, industrial marketing, services marketing, competitor analysis, and the like. These are courses that often include a project or other activity where students must gather data or make recommendations about data gathering. You've often wished there was a book you could assign as supplemental reading that would help students think about how to gather market data (including where to find additional information on specific research techniques). Until this book you faced the unpalatable alternatives of (1) expecting them to find on their own a comprehensive market research textbook and read the appropriate sections (because you can't assume that your students have necessarily taken a market research course);

or (2) hoping they will find, assemble, and read specialist volumes on focus groups, surveys, and so forth, and then make an intelligent choice among them; or (3) scheduling enough office hours to help students work through the above issues.

The Sage Publications Web site includes a set of resources for instructors. Here you will find a sample syllabus for a market research course, recommended cases along with a suggested teaching approach, and a set of PowerPoint slides that can be used as a basis for developing lectures. If you do assign this book in your class, I'd be interested to hear about your experiences—E-mail me at emcquarrie@scu.edu.

Working Professional Student. You need an overview of market research that can be quickly grasped, a set of tips and cautions to help you through your initial efforts, and advice on where to go to learn more.

Acknowledgments

I received all of my training in market research "in the field," and I'd like to acknowledge some of the individuals and firms from whom I learned the most. Particular thanks go to Nick Calo, Mike Kuhn, Ron Tatham, and many others at Burke Marketing Research, where I got my start moderating focus groups and doing copy tests of advertisements; to Dave Stewart of the University of Southern California and Bill BonDurant of Hewlett-Packard's Market Research and Information Center, for introducing me to best practices in the planning of market research; to Lew Jamison and Karen Thomas at Sun Microsystems, for inviting me to design a course on market research, and thus giving me the confidence to attempt this book; to the editor for the first edition, Marquita Flemming at Sage, for actually giving me the impetus; to Al Bruckner at Sage, editor for the second edition, for encouraging a revision; to Klaus Hoffmann and Tomas Lang, of HP Marketing Education in Europe, for the initial opportunity to teach marketing research to managers; to Shelby McIntyre of Santa Clara University, for many insights into effective market research; and to my clients at Apple Computer, Cadence Design, CIGNA, Compaq, Fluke, Harris, Hewlett-Packard, Microsoft, Motorola, Sun Microsystems, Tektronix, and elsewhere, for challenging questions concerning the application of market research to specific business situations.

PART I

1

Nature and Characteristics of Market Research

M arket research is a *marketing* activity, and marketing is a philosophy concerning how to succeed in business. As a philosophy, marketing competes against other philosophies that make different prescriptions for business success. Notable among competitors to the marketing philosophy are the *innovation* philosophy (success comes from technology leadership), the *quality* philosophy (success comes from building the highest quality products), and the *financial* philosophy (success comes from making the most efficient use of resources). As a philosophy, marketing argues for the primary importance of focusing on markets and customers to guide business decisions. From this perspective, market research consists of anything and everything the firm does to learn about and understand markets and customers. Adherents to the marketing philosophy are distinguished by their willingness to grant prime authority to market facts and customer needs when choosing among courses of action. Practitioners of other philosophies do not so much ignore markets and customers as relegate them to a secondary role, as two among many checkpoints, to be consulted toward the end rather than the beginning of decision making.

Because market research reflects a particular business philosophy, and because this philosophy focuses on learning, organizational change may be required when a firm desires to improve its performance with respect to market research. Put another way, to be truly effective, market research cannot be treated as an isolated function assigned to specialized staff. It has to be a cultural orientation that suffuses the organization.

The literature on organizational learning is pertinent here (Barabba and Zaltman, 1991; Day, 1994a, 1994b). If the goal is to be constantly learning about markets and customers, then a wide variety of business functions, and individuals occupying a variety of job roles, have to become involved in market research. Otherwise, information on markets and customers accumulates in nooks and crannies across the firm, but this information fails to influence decisions.

In light of the above, this book has been written to make key ideas about market research accessible to a wider audience. The guiding metaphor is that there exists a toolbox of market research techniques. Many homeowners have a toolbox in the house, although few would present themselves as carpenters. Similarly, many managers need a basic understanding of market research even though market research does not appear in their job descriptions. Just as many homeowners can use a hammer effectively, without being able to build a house, so also many managers need to understand what descriptive survey research can (and cannot) do. The next section of this chapter opens the toolbox to show the major compartments of the toolbox. This introductory chapter then concludes with some limiting cases, the better to set the scope of market research. The next chapter outlines a process for designing and planning market research.

Distinction 1: Marketing Intelligence Versus Market Research Project

Market research projects involve efforts sharply bounded in space and time and expressly linked to some project such as development of a new product. These studies have a clear beginning and end, and their cost is assigned to an individual project budget. Virtually all of the techniques whose names are common knowledge among businesspeople—the questionnaire, the focus group, the experiment—are applied as part of market research studies. Marketing intelligence, by contrast, is an ongoing activity not tied solely to a specific project. As the root metaphor suggests, marketing intelligence consists of bits and pieces of information gained from agents in the field, from diverse publications, from having your ear to the ground, and so forth; often these bits and pieces have been extensively sifted by expert judgment.

For market intelligence gathering, the core competence required for success is one part database management and one part organizational leadership. It takes vision for a firm's management to commit resources to the gathering of market intelligence not tied directly to any specific project budget. A minimally adequate effort would involve maintaining a library where reports bought by subscription from consultants such as the Gartner Group, DataQuest, IDC, and so forth, are filed. Over time, more and more of these resources have become available online so that they can be accessed at the individual manager's desktop. Still to come are database systems that combine published reports with the firm's own reports of past market research studies and with more diverse kinds of intelligence, such as trip reports from customer visits. Only now are free-form text databases developing to the point where masses of amorphous marketing intelligence can be collated, searched, and sifted. We may expect that Customer Relationship Management software will increasingly be adapted to this purpose.

The challenge posed to software skills, computer network design, and expert systems by the imperative to collect and collate massive amounts of marketing intelligence should not be minimized. Nonetheless, I suspect the greater barrier to improving the availability and quality of marketing intelligence in the typical firm will consist of organizational and cultural factors. Information is power, and information is wealth. Wealth and power are never lightly shared. Thus, how freely does the sales force share information on customers? Who is allowed to see the results of a market research study? Who (if anyone) is charged and incentivized with bringing together information from disparate sources? These are the sorts of issues that confront an executive who wants to improve the caliber of marketing intelligence available within a firm.

For market research studies, the core competence is problem formulation skills. Most business situations do not present themselves as clearly delineated problems but as tangled messes that might be approached in a variety of ways. As will be developed in the next chapter, to succeed in a market research study requires that the sponsoring manager clearly articulate the decision to be addressed and the specific kinds of information needed. Most of the other skills needed to complete a market research study (i.e., expertise in sample selection, experimental design, and statistical analysis) can be purchased from outside vendors. But the correct formulation of the research question ultimately resides with the sponsoring manager. Although good consultants can assist in formulating problems, the authority to determine the real underlying problem inevitably remains with the executive who has profit/loss responsibility for the product or service in question.

Distinction 2: Exploratory Versus Confirmatory Research

Any particular market research study can be categorized as exploratory or confirmatory in intent. The goal of exploratory market research is *discovery.* The underlying questions are What's new? And what are we missing? The goal of confirmatory techniques is *resolution:* Is this the right choice? What specific results can we expect? You conduct exploratory market research to open your eyes and broaden your vision. You conduct confirmatory research to narrow your options and concentrate your efforts along the optimal path.

Exploratory techniques tend to coincide with information needs early in the decision cycle, whereas confirmatory techniques come into play later on. Here "decision cycle" refers to the set of decisions made over the course of a project. "Projects" would include the development of a new product, an investigation of whether a market should be segmented into submarkets, an inquiry into whether to concentrate on a particular niche, an assessment of customer satisfaction, and so forth.

The distinction between exploratory and confirmatory techniques is absolutely crucial. As will be explained when we discuss the individual techniques, all the factors that make a market research technique useful in an exploratory context tend to render it highly suspect in a confirmatory context. Stories are legion of the misuse of exploratory techniques (i.e., the focus group) to obtain a degree of certainty that can only be achieved by more expensive and arduous means. It is equally a mistake to use confirmatory techniques when discovery is the goal. Although the misuse of exploratory techniques incurs direct costs in the form of wrong or suboptimal decisions, the misuse of confirmation techniques tends to incur opportunity costs. When confirmatory techniques are misapplied, discoveries fail to occur, alternatives go unrecognized, and insight is not achieved. If you make hasty use of confirmatory techniques too early in the decision cycle, you run the risk of getting wonderfully precise answers—to the wrong questions.

It is useful to distinguish between relatively exploratory and relatively confirmatory forms of *both* market intelligence gathering and market research studies. Here are examples of each:

Market intelligence, exploratory. Once a month you log on to a database such as Dialog or a search site such as Google and perform a keyword search for every mention in any article of each of your three largest competitors. These articles are reviewed for possible insights into competitive strategy.

Market intelligence, confirmatory. You subscribe to a service that monitors sales in or shipments to some particular distribution channel. Results are periodically analyzed in terms of sales trends for the channel, changes in market share for yourself and competitors, and so forth.

Market research, exploratory. You conduct focus groups to get a better grasp of how your brand is regarded, relative to key competitors, in a certain market segment.

Market research, confirmatory. You conduct a survey of 1,000 customers to assess perceptions of your brand relative to the competition on each of eight significant performance attributes.

As shown by these examples, market intelligence efforts generally provide data that can be analyzed in a variety of different ways or that will be relevant to multiple projects or decisions. The theme again is that a considerable amount of human judgment has to be supplied in order to derive the expected benefits from the data collection. Of course, judgment is also required to get the best results from market research studies, but much of that judgment gets exercised up front in the design of the research study. Market intelligence data allow for more opportunistic analyses, whereas analysis of market research studies is more constrained by the initial design.

All four examples just given focus on issues of competitive standing. Of course, this is far from the only possible focus for market intelligence and market research. Broadly speaking, market intelligence and market research studies can be focused on either *markets* or *customers.* Customers are individual human beings with feelings, perceptions, opinions, and reactions—customers make decisions and experience reactions. Markets are aggregates consisting of groups, institutions, resource flows, environmental forces, and contexts. Markets grow or shrink in size, concentrate or fragment, become more competitive or less so, or change quickly or slowly. Market research focused on customers typically draws on the discipline of psychology, whereas research on markets relies more on theories drawn from economics and sociology. To give some sense of the difference in emphasis, here are four more examples, all of which concentrate on customers rather than on competition (competition is an aspect of markets):

> *Market intelligence, exploratory.* Whenever a customer visit occurs, the person making the visit always asks the customer, "If you could change any one thing about this product, what would that be?" Answers are logged in a text database and reviewed quarterly.

> *Market intelligence, confirmatory.* You subscribe to a survey that periodically measures buying intentions for your product and others.

> *Market research, exploratory.* You conduct 24 customer visits to identify problems and needs that should be addressed when you design the next generation of an existing instrument product.

> *Market research, confirmatory.* You conduct an experiment to determine which of three pricing levels provides the optimum combination of market share and profit margin for a new product.

The distinctions between marketing intelligence and market research projects, exploratory or confirmatory intent, and market versus customer data are useful for organizing the domain of market research. Most of the remainder of this book focuses on the tools used in market research projects; marketing intelligence receives less emphasis. The exploratory versus confirmatory distinction is central to many of the recommendations offered, and the collection of data on both markets and customers is discussed. Before describing the process of planning a market research project, this introduction concludes with a discussion of the scope of market research. Two questions that often arise are (1) Which comes first, business strategy or market research? and (2) What is the role of market research in facilitating the commercialization of true innovations?

Business Strategy

Market Research

Figure 1.1   Reciprocal Relationship of Business Strategy and Market Research

Relationship of Business Strategy to Market Research

Business strategy involves a goal and a plan for achieving that goal. Strategies can be differentiated according to both the goal and the plan. Thus, two typical but very different goals would be to maximize profitability on a quarter-by-quarter basis, or to maximize market share over a multiyear time frame. Examples of typical but distinct plans (any of which could be appropriate with respect to several different strategic goals) would be to achieve low-cost leadership in production processes, to build strong brands, to pursue innovative solutions, to offer unique product functionality, and so forth. Aaker (2004) provides a handy compendium of different kinds of business strategies along with frameworks for integrating and differentiating the various business strategies in use today.

Given this definition, it can be argued that in principle market research and business strategy have a reciprocal relationship, as shown in Figure 1.1. Sometimes market research comes *after* business strategy (this is probably the most common sequence). That is, first a plan is hatched in the minds of management, and second, market research is conducted to determine the odds of success with respect to each alternative approach to implementing the plan (and what can be done to improve these odds). However, it is equally possible for market research to precede and to provide input to the formulation of business strategy. At a time of transition in the business, management may choose to embark first on an intensive examination of markets and customers, and second, to formulate new strategies. In successful firms we expect to see an ongoing dynamic relationship between business strategy and market research. Ideas are conceived and then refined through specific market research projects, while at the same time ongoing market research yields up new ideas for gaining strategic advantage.

However, it can be argued that firms that are relatively more market oriented place proportionately greater influence on the *strategy discovery* function of market research, whereas firms that are relatively less market oriented tend to emphasize the *strategy confirmation* function. This argument rests on the idea that if a firm's business strategies seldom originate from market research, then this is probably a firm that is not primarily focused on markets and customers—that is, not market oriented. An interesting extension of this argument is that market-oriented firms in general, and firms concerned with discovering or generating strategies in particular, can be expected to place more emphasis on, and invest extra effort in, the more exploratory and qualitative techniques of market research (e.g., customer visits, focus groups).

Finally, I would argue that the more challenging and difficult task occurs when market research precedes and is intended to lead to formulation of a new business strategy. When instead market research is used to implement an existing strategy, the challenges are primarily technical, heavier reliance can be placed on outsiders and specialists, and the interpretation of research results is more straightforward. Conversely, market research in the service of strategy generation requires greater involvement by decision makers and presents more difficult conceptual challenges, and its results require more effort to interpret effectively.

Technological Innovation and Market Research

In some engineering circles market research is regarded with suspicion as an inherently conservative activity with a built-in bias against anything really new. If you have engaged in this dialogue, as I have on numerous occasions, you know that this accusation is almost always followed by a telling anecdote intended to clinch the argument. The birth of Apple Computer is a favorite example: we know that Steve Jobs and Steve Wozniak did no formal market research whatsoever prior to launching the product that kicked off the enormous personal computer market. Further, it is somewhat hilarious to imagine an innocent citizen in 1977 receiving a phone call from a market researcher who asks a series of questions along the lines of "Do you need a computer at home for your personal use? What would be the most important application for this computer? How large a memory should it have?" With a glint in his eye our sparring partner will fold his arms and conclude, "There— if the founders of Apple Computer had done market research, the Apple II would never have been introduced, they'd be millions of dollars poorer, and a very useful tool would have seen its diffusion into society woefully retarded."

Many anecdotes similar to the story of Apple Computer are readily available. You may even encounter a particularly sophisticated debater who attempts a one-two punch by bringing in the devastating failure (at least initially) that attended the introduction of New Coke in 1984. New Coke provides the converse story: We know that millions of dollars were spent on market research and we know that Coca-Cola is among the most successful companies in the world, indicating that that market research was probably ably conducted. Nonetheless, this intensive market research effort still could not prevent an embarrassing failure.

These anecdotes would appear to confirm two truths: that successful innovation can occur without market research, and that the presence of market research does not guarantee innovation success. From here our debating partner wants to jump to the next conclusion: "Therefore, market research is generally a waste of time for technology companies." For further support, our debating partner points to the rapid pace of change in technology, the sheer complexity of technological products, and the inability of customers to articulate or even envision how they would use something that doesn't yet exist, as explanations for why market research is ineffectual when technological innovation is the goal.

Of course, anecdotes really are not very effective tools of argument. You come up with a success story where market research was not done, and I respond with a different anecdote where market research played a crucial role. Neither of us persuades the other. To move forward, a debate like this needs good research, comprising a large number of cases, that would allow us to estimate the relative frequency of instances where market research proved crucial to success, versus the relative frequency of cases where it proved superfluous. In fact, such research *has* been conducted and has accumulated for decades (see Suggested Readings at the end of this chapter). The results are unambiguous: when we step back from individual war stories to the aggregate level, and examine large numbers of innovations, or compare large numbers of successful versus failed new products, we find that a majority of the success stories are characterized by disciplined efforts to understand customers and markets, whereas a majority of the failures exhibit a neglect of or incompetence in market research.

Those are the facts: *on average,* successful new product development efforts include more market research, conducted more effectively, and performed earlier in the development process, whereas *on average* failed new products exhibit the reverse profile. These facts accommodate any anecdote our sparring partner may produce. Because the claim is only that market research is useful *on average,* we can readily acknowledge instances where market research does no good or fails to prevent harm. Apple Computer and New Coke are not the first and will not be the last such examples. Ultimately it comes down to a question of odds: do you want to gamble that your company, your technology, and your project are among the exceptions where market research happens to be a waste of time? I would suggest that your stockholders would very much prefer that you play the percentages, and direct your energies to the question of what specific kind of market research would do you the most good in your particular situation, and not to a misguided effort to succeed without the aid of any kind of market research.

So, you might be wondering, what kind of market research is most suitable when the goal is a commercially successful technological innovation? This question is addressed at greater length in Chapter 12 on applications of research, but it may be useful to sketch out an answer here. First, we have to acknowledge that innovations may be more or less radical, or discontinuous relative to prior offerings. Given this distinction, the following rules of thumb can be applied:

1. The less radical the innovation, the broader the set of market research tools that may be relevant.

At the extreme, when the innovation might better be described as "version 2.0" of an existing product, virtually any of the techniques discussed in this book may be applicable at some point in the process.

2. The more radical the innovation, the greater the pertinence of qualitative market research techniques (e.g., customer visits and focus groups).

As we shall see, quantitative market research techniques, (e.g., survey, conjoint analysis) typically presume a high degree of knowledge on the part of management (so that highly specific questions can be devised) and a good deal of familiarity with the product category or domain on the part of customers (so that they can answer specific questions). Both of these are lacking in the case of radical innovation.

3. There do exist innovations, typically radical, where market research of almost any kind is premature, not cost-justified, or of limited value.

Sometimes the very best market research consists of introducing the product and carefully observing what initially transpires. In this case market research makes its contribution after the innovation is introduced, with the aim of maximizing the odds of commercial success. In such cases, the market research doesn't really contribute to configuring the innovation per se, but rather addresses such questions as identifying the most receptive target audience, calibrating the price point, selecting the most effective message strategy, and the like. None of these constitutes the innovation itself, but any one might be a crucial determinant of whether the innovation is commercially successful.

Concluding Comments

The preceding topics, in addition to their intrinsic interest, serve to reveal the author's bias. It is important to foreground this bias because it shapes the entire treatment of the book. Simply put, I think that qualitative market research techniques are underutilized and underappreciated, relative to confirmatory, quantitative techniques. As a result, this book, unlike most general treatments of market research, places substantial emphasis on qualitative techniques. Thus, if one were to pick up the typical academic textbook (see Suggested Readings for some respected examples), and counted pages to determine the relative importance of topics, you might infer that factor analyses were a more important component of commercial market research than focus groups, or that discriminant analyses featured in more market research studies than interviews. In fact, these are specialized statistical techniques that have their place, but that are rather more likely to be seen in academic than in commercial research contexts.

There are good historical and sociological reasons for the relative neglect of qualitative market research techniques. First of all, the path to promotion and prestige in academic social science rests on the ability to master arcane statistical analyses. Ph.D. programs in marketing and in supporting disciplines such as psychology and economics heavily emphasize training in statistics and associated mathematical subjects such as probability theory. The best journals feature the most elaborate and advanced statistical treatments. Publication in such journals is the sine qua non for promotion and tenure. As a result, most instructors teaching market research, particularly those teaching in the better graduate programs, owe much of their own career success to their facility with and mastery of statistical analysis. It should come as no surprise if their course syllabi and the textbooks they choose also emphasize the analysis of quantitative market research data.

Another factor contributing to the minimal coverage accorded to qualitative research techniques in textbooks and courses is the sheer abundance of statistical techniques that have some relevance to market research. There really are dozens of statistical techniques like factor analysis, each associated with a substantial literature, and each sufficiently complex that an adequate explanation requires a 20- to 40-page chapter. The instructor who feels responsible for covering as much as possible of the domain of market research as reflected in the textbook ("I can't send these future managers into the world ignorant of the benefits of multidimensional scaling") inevitably ends up slighting qualitative research. For, in contrast to the abundance of techniques for statistical analyses, there are only a handful of qualitative research techniques, and most of these involve some kind of interview.

A third factor is particularly apropos to one of the key target audiences for this book—managers responsible for technology businesses. In most technology firms, especially those that sell business to business, management staff consists of engineers and scientists. These are people whose career success may initially have rested on their mastery of the intricacies of the physics that underlie electrical engineering. As scientifically and technically trained individuals, these managers understand the power of quantification and the virtues of the scientific method. As managers socialized into contemporary American business culture, these people are also likely to espouse a management science approach to business decision making. This background leads quite naturally to a demand that market researchers deliver precise numerical estimates: What is the size of this market? How fast is it growing? How many dollars can we charge for this feature? Only quantitative market research techniques can answer such questions.

Unfortunately, training in the physical sciences is not always a good preparation for training in the social sciences (ask any instructor of engineers newly enrolled in an MBA program!). Human data are different from physical data. Most notably, measurements on humans are subject to much greater uncertainty than measurements taken on things, and are much more mutable—what is true today may not be true tomorrow, and what is true for this customer may not be true for another customer. Qualitative techniques are ideally suited to grappling with uncertainty and novelty. (This is why these techniques are particularly pertinent in the case of discontinuous technological innovation.) When the issue is not What's the answer? but rather What's the question?, qualitative and exploratory techniques came into their own.

In summary, the discipline needs a market research book that corrects for the unequal and subordinate emphasis typically placed on qualitative techniques, and the target audience for this book is in particular need of education in the potential benefits of qualitative research. That is, technology managers are generally less familiar with nonquantified but disciplined social science research. Perhaps more important, quantitative market research techniques are often unsuitable for technology markets, inasmuch as they may presume a sample drawn from a large homogeneous population (technology markets are often fragmented and small), easy-to-explain product functionality (technology products are complex), and a stable competitive and pricing environment (technology markets change rapidly). All of these factors play to the strength of qualitative techniques.

Now that you've been introduced to the topic of market research and alerted to the author's biases, we can turn to the fundamental responsibility of managers with respect to market research: planning.

References and Suggested Readings

Aaker, David. 2004. *Strategic Market Management,* 7th ed. New York: Wiley.

> This short book provides a brief introduction to the range of strategies and strategy frameworks in use today.

Barabba, Vincent P., and Gerald Zaltman. 1991. *Hearing the Voice of the Market.* Cambridge, MA: Harvard Business School Press.

> This book emphasizes marketing intelligence and how to institutionalize, within the corporate organization, best practices in the use of market information.

Bonnet, D. C. L. 1986. Nature of the R&D/marketing cooperation in the design of technologically advanced new industrial products. *R&D Management* 16: 117–126.

> Bonnet reviews studies subsequent to Utterman (see below) yielding similar results.

Cooper, Robert G. 1993. *Winning of New Products: Accelerating the Process from Idea to Launch.* Cambridge, MA: Addison-Wesley.

> Cooper provides a review of studies of new product success and failure and discusses best practices at each stage of development.

Day, George S. 1994a. The capabilities of market driven organizations. *Journal of Marketing* 58 (October): 37–52.

Day, George S. 1994b. Continuous learning about markets. *California Management Review* 36(4): 9–31.

> The first article provides an integration of current thinking about where market research fits among other market capabilities, and a good guide to the literature on market orientation and its contribution to profitability. The second article discusses what an organization committed to gathering marketing intelligence would do.

Utterback, J. M. 1974. Innovation and the diffusion of technology. *Science* 183: 620–626.

Utterback is the classic source on technology-push vs. demand-pull paths to successful innovation.

The following publications provide a means of keeping up with developments in market research.

Journal of Advertising Research (JAR) emphasizes research on all aspects of advertising, has a strong practitioner focus, and often reports studies based on real-world data.

Journal of Marketing Research (JMR) is the leading academic journal in this area. Highly technical articles emphasize tests of theories and new analytic techniques.

Journal of the Market Research Society (JMRS) is a leading British journal that has historically been strong in the area of qualitative research.

Journal of Product Innovation Management (JPIM) is the best source for current thinking on new product development.

Marketing News (MN) is the newsletter of the American Marketing Association and regularly publishes guides to market research software, focus group facilities, and so forth.

Marketing Research Magazine (MR) is addressed to practitioners and provides many detailed examples of the actual market research practices and policies of leading firms.

Marketing Science (MS) is a prestigious academic journal that emphasizes the development and testing of mathematical models of marketing phenomena such as price elasticity and effects of various budget levels.

2

Planning for Market Research

Decision Problem to Research Question

The first step in planning a market research study is to spend some time identifying and articulating the underlying decision problem that makes a research study seem necessary. The importance of this initial step cannot be overemphasized. The more secure the researcher's grasp of the decision problem, the greater the probability that the results of market research will make a difference and contribute real value to the firm. Conversely, when the decision problem is left tacit or never developed, the research effort may be misguided, or may address only part of the problem or even the wrong problem altogether. This is to reiterate that market research is conducted to serve the needs of business decision makers. If this imperative is lost sight of, then research activities may simply be an expensive way to satisfy idle curiosity, an exercise in politics (to justify decisions already made), or an excuse for dithering and failing to take action.

This prescription to articulate the decision problem at the beginning may sound straightforward, but it is surprisingly difficult to implement in practice. One difficulty is that the person responsible for designing and implementing the market research study is generally not the same individual as the decision maker who must act on the research results. This separation of responsibilities makes communication failures all too likely. If the researcher does not spend enough time in dialogue with the decision maker, the full dimensions of the decision problem may not come into view. When this happens, the decision maker is likely to be disappointed with the results of the research, finding them to be either beside the point or only half an answer.

Even when the decision maker and researcher are the same individual, it is still important to spend some time articulating the decision problem prior to specifying the market research study. The reason is that most decision makers do not face isolated, clearly defined problems. Instead, they face tangled messes. Thus, a decision maker may find him- or herself thinking,

> Sales fell short last year. But sales would have approached the goal, except for six territories in two regions, where results were very poor. Of course, we implemented an across-the-board price increase last year, so our profit margin goals were just about met, even though sales revenue fell short. Yet, two of our competitors saw above-trend sales increases last year. Still, another competitor seems to be struggling, and word on the street is they have been slashing prices to close deals. Of course, the economy was pretty uneven across our geographies last year. . . .

Simultaneously our decision maker is grappling with the dissonant views and varying agendas of colleagues and peers. One colleague takes the sales shortfall as an opportunity to push once more for an expansion of the product line; another reiterates that the alignment of sales incentives with sales performance goals has not been reviewed in years, and that one of the regions in question saw considerable turnover in the sales force last year. About that point, our decision maker's own manager may pop in with a reminder that a revised sales forecast is due at the end of the quarter. What a mess!

In short, whether or not the researcher and decision maker are the same individual, time must be spent and the effort made to identify the focal decision problem. Once the decision problem has been stated, we can make an intelligent decision about whether to do a market research at all, and if so, which technique to use. If the decision problem is not articulated, then the organization either does not do any market research, blundering forward as best it can, or defaults to whatever research technique is either traditional within the firm ("Let's send customers a questionnaire") or the personal favorite approach of some key manager ("Focus groups would be good here"). I cannot emphasize this point strongly enough: it is impossible to make an intelligent selection from among the many market research techniques available, absent a clear and comprehensive formulation of the decision problem the research is supposed to address.

Table 2.1 outlines a process for identifying decision problems and translating these into a research design. Returning to our "sales are

Table 2.1   Planning Process for Marketing Research

Stage	Issues to Be Resolved
1. Identify and articulate the decision problem	• Who is the decision maker? • What are alternative ways to state the problem? • Do these statements get at the problem or are they only symptoms of some deeper problem? • Is this a decision that can be addressed through market research?
2. Identify key questions that must be answered before a decision can be made	• What specific questions are most pertinent? • Is there one question or many questions? • Can this question be answered with the time and money available?
3. Identify research techniques that would be appropriate for answering these questions	• One research technique or several? • Techniques used in combination or in sequence?
4. Design the research study	• What specific objectives should guide the research? • Who should participate (i.e., if primary research, how many of what kind of customers; if secondary research, what data sources should be consulted) • Estimate needed budget, time frame, and other resource requirements

down" example, and assuming that the decision maker has been identified, the next step is to generate alternative statements of the decision problem. Here are some examples of alternative formulations of the decision problem:

1. We need to overhaul our sales compensation system. What changes should we make?

2. Our product line has to be broadened. What expansions would be best?

3. We have to improve the price-performance ratio of our offering to make it more effective. Should we adjust price, add services, or do both?

4. We need to diagnose what went wrong in the six lagging sales territories and identify corrective actions.

Each of these problem statements can be mapped onto the decision maker's musings reproduced earlier. However, each statement is going to take us in a very different direction as far as conducting any market research is concerned. In fact, at least one of these decision problems (the sales compensation issue) can't be addressed by market research as conventionally understood. True, some sort of investigation may be conducted in this instance (as when we gather information on the compensation practices of other firms in our industry for purposes of benchmarking), but market research, at least from the perspective of this book, should not be confused with the broader category of social science research, or the even broader activity of fact-gathering in general. Market research, as we shall use the term, refers to a specific set of information gathering activities focused on customers or markets. Thus, problem statements 2, 3, or 4 can be addressed through some kind of market research, as defined in this book, whereas problem statement 1 cannot. In other words, one of the first fruits of attempting to formulate alternative problem statements may be the realization that market research is beside the point. If decision makers have other information that suggests that the sales compensation system is out of whack, and that this misalignment is beginning to hurt company performance, they may well choose to nominate that problem as *the* problem, and attack it first, without getting involved in market research per se.

Can we now choose which of the remaining formulations represents the *best* statement of the decision problem at hand? In the abstract, as an outside researcher having only the information reproduced in these pages, there really is no way to determine which of the remaining statements represents the best formulation—only the decision maker knows. That is, the decision maker possesses a great deal of other knowledge, both explicit and tacit, that is essential for selecting which of the remaining statements should be used to guide market research. Until the decision maker weighs all the information available and comes to a conclusion such as "I'm really worried that we're not price competitive," or "My hunch is that the sales problem is local to those half a dozen territories," the design of market research cannot proceed.

In the abstract, any of the remaining statements could be *the* problem statement (and these are far from an exhaustive list). Each statement is capable of guiding subsequent market research, each captures at least some of the uncertainty facing the decision maker, and each is plausible as a response to the triggering complaint—sales are down.

The discussion thus far suggests several practical insights into the conduct of market research. First, if the researcher and decision maker are not the same person, then it is imperative that the researcher have some kind of significant dialogue with the decision maker. The decision maker has to decide what the problem is, and in the real world, beset by complicated messes and the competing agendas of colleagues, this is no easy task. Hence, to be effective, market researchers cannot simply be order takers ("Four focus groups, coming right up"). Order takers fail their clients, because to be effective, good researchers have to help clients think through the problems at hand. Order takers also fail in their own business because the model is flawed—successful researchers have to be consultants, not order takers. If the decision maker and researcher are one and the same person, then the decision maker must conduct this Socratic dialogue with him- or herself, first generating alternative problem statements and then selecting the best candidate among them.

Second, it should be apparent that each of the remaining problem statements leads to very different sorts of market research efforts. Thus, a focus on broadening the product line may not delve deeply into pricing issues or involve a comparison and contrast of specific sales territories. What may be less apparent is that every alternative problem statement foregrounds or privileges some possible answer to the triggering complaint, and backgrounds or excludes other potential answers or resolutions. If we choose to focus our research on the six lagging territories, we are implicitly rejecting the idea that there is anything wrong with our product line per se. In selecting a problem formulation, we may be mistaken (after all, we haven't conducted any research as yet!), and this mistake may not be recoverable in the time available. There is no way to escape this dilemma. It serves as a reminder that problem formulation has to be done carefully. If we get the problem right, then some kind of market research will probably be helpful. If we get the problem wrong, it won't matter how good the research is.

To return to Table 2.1, let's suppose that the decision maker has a strong hunch that there really is a localized problem in the six territories—or at least, wants to rule this out before proceeding to any other investigations. Once we have settled on a decision problem, as captured in statement 4, the next step is to brainstorm the kinds of questions that have to be answered before corrective actions can be undertaken. For example, are the six lagging territories distinctive in some other way, relative to the remaining territories, beyond the difference in sales growth? Do the six territories share any common factors that are uncommon among the remaining territories? If we could find other shared differences or commonalities, we can examine these as potential causes for the sales shortfall in these territories.

Given questions of this sort, we can ask whether they are answerable at a reasonable cost, and begin to identify an appropriate research technique. Note again that once we accept a problem formulation that focuses on the six problematic sales territories, we cease to ask questions about differences that are general across the firm's markets, such as our price performance ratio, or problems with product line breadth.

As phrased, the question about factors shared by the six territories, that in turn distinguish them from other sales territories, seems eminently answerable. We may assume that the firm maintains one or more databases containing descriptive data on each territory. External databases should also be available, allowing us to ask about the overall economic health or growth rate of each of territory, population factors associated with each territory, and so on.

It would appear, then, that our initial selection of research technique will be to gather and also tap into existing sources of marketing intelligence. To name this approach as a technique, whenever we gather marketing intelligence to address a specific decision we can refer to this as "secondary research." We design a secondary research effort by specifying the kinds of archived data we wish to examine and the specific variables we will analyze, in this case, for the purpose of comparing the six territories with the remainder. Thus, we will look to internal databases for data on sales calls undertaken, the ratio of wins to losses, sales force turnover in each territory, and so forth. We will consult external databases for information on competitor presence and activity in each territory, economic factors affecting each territory, and so forth.

At this point the research design is essentially complete. We have formulated the decision problem, generated specific research questions to be addressed, and selected an appropriate research technique capable of addressing these questions. What remains is to implement the research, analyze and interpret the results, and formulate corrective actions (which in some cases may themselves need to be vetted by additional research). To complete the loop, one of two outcomes is likely in the case of our running example. On the one hand, analysis of secondary data may produce a "smoking gun." For instance, we may discover that the struggling competitor, who slashed prices last year, has a strong presence in each of the six lagging territories, but has much less of a presence in most of the remaining territories. We now have a potential explanation for the overall sales shortfall, and can begin to generate potential managerial responses. These might include authorizing a higher level of discount when going head to head with this competitor, or more heavily promoting those aspects of our product's functionality where this competitor's product is weakest, and so on.

Alternatively, our search for shared commonalities and differences may come up empty. After all, in any given year there will always be six territories at the bottom of the list, and our average sales performance will always look better if we exclude the worst six territories on the list. In other words, the decision maker's hunch may be wrong. Sales growth may have been lower across the board. Perhaps the strong territories were not as strong as they should have been, even as the weakest territories were particularly weak. This outcome will probably lead us to reformulate the decision problem in more general terms, so as to identify corporate-wide factors that could explain the sales shortfall. New research will have to be designed, probably taking the form of some kind of exploratory research involving customers, to get at issues such as breadth of product line, price performance ratio, brand image, and so forth.

Note that this second outcome, in which factors distinguishing the six territories failed to emerge, in no way constitutes a failure of research planning. Given the decision maker's mind-set, industry knowledge, prior expectations, and so forth, it was imperative to investigate the idea that the sales shortfall was fundamentally a local problem. This is particularly the case inasmuch as a relatively quick and inexpensive research process was available to investigate this decision problem (secondary research is typically among the quickest and cheapest of research techniques). We can now more confidently address other formulations of the problem, which are likely to entail more difficult, prolonged, and expensive research.

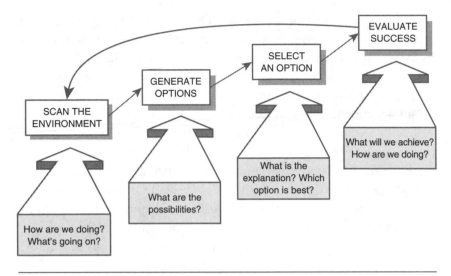

Figure 2.1   The Business Decision Cycle

Types of Decision Problems: The Decision Cycle

As we have just seen, formulating the decision problem is a task that has to be done anew each time that market research is contemplated. The range of researchable decision problems is as wide and various as business itself. (Actually, it's even wider, since nonprofit organizations may also have occasion to do market research.) Nonetheless, it appears that the vast variety of potential decision problems can be clustered into a smaller number of fundamental types. The utility of examining such a typology of decision problems is that it will allow us to make generalizations about the applicability of specific market research tools. The typology may also be useful in guiding our initial efforts at formulating the decision problem in a specific case, insofar as it provides examples of typical decision problems.

Figure 2.1 presents a simple typology of decision problems organized as a cycle that unfolds over time. After this model has been discussed, we will examine the alignment between specific research techniques and specific stages in the decision cycle. The goal in that discussion is to show that once you have located your particular decision within the decision cycle, you will have simultaneously narrowed the range of appropriate research techniques to a small number.

The notion behind the decision cycle is that any major decision—developing a new product or entering a new market, for instance—proceeds through a series of smaller subdecisions. Alternatively, smaller and more localized decisions, such as the problem we worked through in the previous section ("Why are sales down?"), can be situated in the model, and seen in context as representing one kind of a decision rather than another. As a general rule, major decisions such as the development of a new product may require research activities at each stage of the decision cycle. In the case of more minor or localized problems, there may be a single set of research activities, corresponding to a single stage of the decision cycle. The remainder of the decision cycle is then worked through informally without the aid of formal research. Thus, in our running example, if secondary research had shown there to be a specific problem with the six lagging territories, options for addressing the problem might have been generated by management discussion, the best option selected through further discussion, and the results monitored simply by reference to monthly sales figures routinely distributed. Nonetheless, the fundamental supposition underlying Figure 2.1 is that any researchable decision can be logically parsed into four steps, however truncated a particular step might be in practice. Every decision begins with a look at the surrounding context, then proceeds to the generation of decision alternatives, and then proceeds to the selection of one alternative, which then requires an assessment of outcomes, which then segues into a scanning of the environment in preparation for a subsequent decision. Finally, we presume that the distinction of four stages within any decision is consequential for the kinds of research that needs to be done at each stage.

The first stage in the cycle is to *scan the environment*. What's going on? What's out there? This activity of environmental scanning can be thought of as a sharpening and focusing of the activity of intelligence gathering, which, as argued earlier, should be ceaseless. An example of scanning the environment would be to compile analysts' reports on the strategies, strengths, and weaknesses of your major competitors. In this early stage you would probably also examine reports on how the market is segmented, who the biggest users of this product category are, what applications dominate, and so forth.

The second stage in the decision cycle is to *generate options*. What are the possibilities? What specific directions might be worth pursuing?

What choices do we face? For example, if a product line has come to seem aged and tired, there is probably more than one possible approach to rejuvenating it, and all of these need to be identified and explored. If you are seeking to expand your market, you will want to identify all the possible groups that could be targeted for expansion. Likewise, before selecting a new theme for your ad campaign you would want to examine a variety of candidates. Stage two can be thought of as the creative part of the decision cycle. The goal is to broaden your horizons so that you don't neglect opportunities or miss possibilities.

The third stage in the cycle is to critically examine and then *select an alternative* from among those generated in stage two. Which of these options is best? How much will this option achieve for us? It is at this stage that you must decide exactly what functionality a product will offer. This is where you determine which one among several markets is likely to be the largest, or the most lucrative, or the best protected against competitive counterattack. Stage three is crucial because resources are always limited. This is a uniquely stressful stage because you have to commit to one option and abandon the remainder. You may have generated half a dozen attractive alternatives for market expansion, but the lack of money, people, or time will force you to select one or a few on which to concentrate your efforts.

The fourth and final stage is to *evaluate the success* of the decisions you made. How well did we do? Did we take market share away from the competitor we targeted? Did the new ad campaign change attitudes among the intended audience? How satisfied are customers who bought the new product? Results from the fourth stage are added to the stock of market intelligence possessed by the firm. These results also influence management's ongoing strategic review of business directions. Recalling Figure 1.1 in Chapter 1 and the reciprocal influence between strategy and market research, we can think of the entire decision cycle as occurring within the context of ongoing strategic review. In business, decisions never stop.

Matching Tools to Decisions

A central purpose of this model of the decision cycle is to help you decide which market research tools might be useful at any given point.

To do this requires a third concept that can bridge the gap between decision stages on the one hand and the market research toolbox on the other. Here the concept of a *research objective* is helpful. A research objective states, in a single sentence, what result you hope to achieve through the use of some particular research technique. An example might be, "Identify areas of satisfaction and dissatisfaction with our current product offering." Good research objectives always start with an action verb. If you leave out the verb, you end up with something vague and empty—a wish, hope, or yearning.

Articulating your objective in this concise and concrete way has two benefits. First, it forces you to stop and think: really, what kind of information do I need, given my formulation of the decision problem? This is a nontrivial benefit. Although a decision problem has been articulated, this problem was extracted from a mess, and that mess tends to reappear, in the form of a wide range of poorly articulated issues and queries. Most managers are buffeted by numerous conflicting deadlines, interruptions, sudden changes of course, and the like. A requirement to spell out the specific information desired from this market research expenditure usefully concentrates the mind.

A second benefit of spelling out your objective is that you often discover that the objective you have just written out is insufficient—it reflects only part of what you are trying to accomplish. In conceptual terms, articulating research objectives represents a continuation and intensification of the initial attempt to formulate the decision problem. To continue the example given above, you may well realize that your actual objective is more comprehensive, and better corresponds to this two-part statement: (1) Identify areas of satisfaction and dissatisfaction. (2) Prioritize areas of dissatisfaction according to degree of negative impact on revenue. Having reached this point, you may next realize that the research procedures required to *identify* areas of dissatisfaction may not be the same as those required to *prioritize* them. To identify requires an exploratory approach that can uncover what exists; to prioritize requires a precise and confirmatory approach that can take a set of existing things and order them from best to worst or most to least. With that realization you are well on your way to articulating a research strategy encompassing multiple data collection activities that holds some promise of meeting all your information needs with respect to the decision problem at hand.

Table 2.2   Examples of Research Objectives

Verb	Some Possible Objects
1. Identify:	Problems, opportunities, choice criteria . . .
2. Define:	Concept, design, potential . . .
3. Describe:	Decision process, usage, work environment . . .
4. Explore:	Perceptions, reactions, remedies . . .
5. Generate:	Hypotheses, alternatives, explanations . . .
6. Evaluate:	Feasibility, attractiveness, potential . . .
7. Select:	Product, concept, ad execution . . .
8. Test:	Preference, direction, profitability . . .
9. Measure:	Growth, size, frequency . . .
10. Prioritize:	Segments, needs, opportunities . . .
11. Monitor:	Trends, competition, events . . .
12. Track:	Spending, satisfaction, awareness . . .

Table 2.2 lists a dozen verbs that often form the basis of research objectives, along with some examples of typical objects for each verb. Thus one can *identify* opportunities or problems or choice criteria, *select* markets or product concepts or ad themes, and so forth. Table 2.2 may not reflect *all* the verbs that provide a useful starting point for formulating market research objectives, but it should cover most situations you will encounter. If you want to use a verb from outside this list, ask yourself whether it really adds anything, and especially whether it is concrete and specific enough. For instance, in my experience a favorite word of businesspeople in the context of market research is "validate." But what does this mean? To validate is to confirm the correctness of some idea we hold, in other words, to test. Whereas "validate" is a long and somewhat unfamiliar word, thus vague in applicability and diffuse in meaning, "test" makes it clear that we are going to attempt to prove the truth of some proposition using fairly rigorous means. With "validate," we could kid ourselves that a dozen customer visits might be enough to validate our ideas, whereas with "test" we are unlikely to convince ourselves or anyone else that a dozen interviews is adequate. Hence, "test" is a more

Table 2.3   Decision Stages, Research Objectives, and Research Tools

| Stage | Objectives | Tools | |
		Primary	Supporting
Scan environment – What's out there? – What's going on?	• Identify • Describe • Monitor	• Secondary research • Customer visits	• Focus groups • Surveys
Generate options – What are the possibilities?	• Generate • Define • Explore	• Customer visits • Focus groups	• Secondary research
Select option – How much will we achieve? – Which one is best?	• Evaluate • Test • Select • Prioritize	• Experiments, surveys • Choice models	• Secondary research
Evaluate outcomes – How well did we do?	• Measure • Track	• Surveys • Secondary research	• Customer visits

useful word because it gives more guidance as to what kind of market research might be able to fulfill our objective. "Validate" blurs the focus of your research planning; "test" sharpens it.

Next, Table 2.3 integrates decision stages, research objectives, and individual research techniques. For each stage, certain research objectives are characteristic and customary. In turn, each research tool plays a primary role in achieving certain objectives and can contribute secondarily to the achievement of others. Table 2.3 is intended to serve several purposes. First, it provides the means to perform a quick check on a research proposal submitted by someone else in your organization. If someone wants to do focus groups in order to *select* which ad execution will have the strongest appeal, a warning light should go off in your mind: focus groups are not listed among the tools used to select an option. Second, Table 2.3 provides a planning and scheduling tool for specifying needed market research over the life of a project. It affords you multiple opportunities to ask questions such as, What activities am I going to undertake so as to scan the environment? or, How will I go about identifying possible new applications for this instrument? A third benefit of Table 2.3 is that it provides three possible entry points to kick off your market research planning. Sometimes you will feel most confident about where you are in the decision cycle; sometimes a particular verb like "identify" or "explore" will be the hook; and sometimes you will be focused on a particular research tool. You can enter Table 2.3 from any of these points and build toward a complete research strategy from that point.

Table 2.4 provides an alternative viewpoint on the relationships mapped in Table 2.3. Now the individual research tools provide the rows and the individual research objectives the columns in a matrix. Where Table 2.3 was decision focused, Table 2.4 is tool focused. It facilitates correct use of each tool via the graphic symbols, which specify that the tool is a primary means of achieving an objective (double check), or contributes secondarily to that objective (single check), or is generally misleading or dangerous in the context of a certain objective (X-mark). Blank cells indicate either that a tool bears little relationship to a certain objective, and hence, no warning is needed, or that it is meaningless to make any overall endorsement or prohibition, because so much depends on how the objective is interpreted in the specific case.

Effective Application of Research Tools

Parts II and III of this book discuss in considerable detail the strengths and weaknesses and best applications and misapplications of individual research tools. However, here it is possible to briefly introduce each tool and simultaneously walk the reader through Tables 2.3 and 2.4. The focus here is on the research objectives and how each tool relates to them; subsequent chapters focus on the tools themselves. The detailed justification for the summary judgments rendered in the discussion below will be deferred until the chapters on individual tools.

To set the stage for this discussion, let me suggest that when considering what kind of market research to do, you are like a carpenter with a toolbox. The toolbox has several compartments, corresponding, for instance, to the distinction between exploratory and confirmatory research. Within each compartment you have the equivalent of a hammer, screwdriver, wrench, saw, and so on. Now imagine if you encountered a homeowner who claimed that he had built his entire house

Table 2.4 Research Tools Matched to Research Objectives

Stages/Objectives

Tool	Scan Environment →			Generate Options →			Select Options →				Evaluate Outcomes	
	Identify	Describe	Monitor	Generate	Define	Explore	Test	Evaluate	Prioritize	Select	Measure	Track
Secondary research	✓✓	✓✓	✓✓	✓	✓	✓	✓	✓	✓	✓	✓✓	✓✓
Customer visits	✓✓	✓✓	✓✓	✓✓	✓✓	✓✓	X	X		X	X	
Focus groups	✓	✓		✓✓	✓✓	✓✓	X	X		X	X	
Survey research	✓	✓✓	✓✓	X	✓	X	✓✓	✓✓	✓✓	✓✓	✓✓	✓✓
Choice models	X					X	✓✓	✓✓	✓✓	✓✓		
Experimentation	X	X		X	X	X	✓✓	✓✓	✓✓	✓✓	✓✓	✓

(Handwritten margin notes beside rows: Qual. — Customer visits; Qual. — Focus groups; Quant. — Survey research; Qual. — Choice models)

Note: A double check indicates that a tool is a superior means of addressing the objective; a single check indicates it is appropriate for pursuing the objective; and an X indicates that the tool is *not* appropriate for this objective. Blanks indicate that the appropriateness or inappropriateness of the tool is uncertain, depending on exactly how the objective is interpreted in a particular context.

using nothing but a nine-inch socket wrench—you would be more appalled than amazed. Why would anyone go through all those contortions when there is an entire toolbox available that has evolved expressly to make house construction as efficient as possible? Yet, it is not uncommon to encounter businesses that, faced with a need for market research, *only* conduct surveys, or *only* do customer visits, or *always* do focus groups. You will be much more effective if you can acquire a sense of the distinctive contribution of each tool together with an understanding of how the tools work together over the course of a project.

To extend the metaphor, have you ever tried to drive in a nail using a screwdriver? It can be done, if you grab the screwdriver by the wrong end and flail away, but the results generally leave much to be desired (and sometimes include breakage or injury). Does this indicate that the screwdriver is a bad tool that ought be chucked out of the toolbox? Of course not. A screwdriver is the wrong tool for driving nails (it is even more difficult to set a screw with a hammer). Every tool in the carpenter's toolbox is adapted to performing a specific task. It is the same with the market research toolbox: each tool is effective in certain applications, and ineffective in others.

SECONDARY MARKET RESEARCH

This research technique encompasses any data collected by someone else for some other purpose that also happens to be useful to you. Secondary research can be composed of internal or external data. Common examples of external secondary research include data compiled by the Census Bureau and other government agencies, reports written by consulting firms and sold to interested parties (e.g., "Five-Year Sales Projections for Color Laser Printers"), and publicly available information, such as articles in the trade press. Common examples of internal secondary research include sales records, customer databases, and past market research reports.

Secondary research has obvious relevance to the environmental scanning stage of the decision cycle. It is almost always quicker and cheaper to answer a question through secondary data than through conducting your own primary market research. In virtually every project your first step should be to amass whatever secondary research is available and glean whatever insights you can. Secondary research can be used to identify market opportunities, describe market structure, and monitor competitive activity. For example, suppose you install and service video cameras used for security purposes. Using secondary research, you might discover that automated teller machines (ATMs) in non-bank locations offer a rapidly growing market for video security. You might encounter this fact in the trade press, or perhaps in a syndicated report on market trends for small video cameras.

Because secondary research comprises so many diverse activities, one or another kind of secondary research may also play a supporting role in both generating *and* selecting options. Thus, a market opportunity identified at an earlier point may be further defined through secondary research. Continuing with our example, secondary research might help you formulate two market expansion options: (1) target large banks with extensive off-premises ATM networks, or (2) target convenience store chains that have recently installed ATMs in their stores. Information on market size or market structure gained through secondary research may also help you evaluate the relative profitability of two different strategic options. Thus, your own internal records may indicate to you that cameras mounted in very small stores require on average more servicing than cameras located in larger buildings. This might be sufficient to cause you to select convenience stores as your initial target market, inasmuch as cameras associated with their new ATMs are likely to generate substantial service revenue.

A particular type of secondary research becomes of primary importance when you reach the fourth stage. Quite often you want to evaluate the outcome of a decision by measuring changes in market share for yourself and key competitors. Syndicated reports (regular studies, produced by independent consulting firms, to which you and other members of your industry subscribe) are often a source of market share data. Alternatively, your own review of secondary data may help you answer this question. Thus, if you can find information on how many ATMs were installed in a region last year, you can compute your share of these installations relative to your goals.

CUSTOMER VISITS

In a program of customer visits, a dozen or more customers are interviewed at their place of business. Customer visits can be thought of as a combination of field research and interviews. Customer visits, along with several other tools, are of primary importance in the environmental scanning stage. Listening to customers describe problems can help to identify new product opportunities. Walking around the customer site facilitates rich descriptions of product applications. Regular contact with customers helps you to monitor emerging market trends and changes in the business environment.

Customer visits are also crucially important, along with focus groups, in the generation of options. This is because the loosely structured nature of these interviews allows for surprises. Similarly, extensive exposure to customers and their way of viewing the world often provides a fresh perspective. Moreover, the intensive dialogue that a two-hour face-to-face interview permits helps you to define issues and explore perceptions in depth.

Customer visits should almost never be used to test, evaluate, or select options. The small sample size, the convenience nature of the sample (i.e., not random), and an unknown degree of interviewer bias makes it impossible to trust the results of customer visits in this connection. (As will be developed subsequently, these same shortcomings are of much less moment when customer visits are used appropriately to scan the environment and generate options.) The lone exception is when you are planning to visit *all* your customers. This might be possible because these customers are all other divisions internal to your firm, or because the market for your product is very limited with only a few large buyers. If you can visit all your customers, then you have a census and not a sample, and the limitations cited above are less pressing. Even here, the portion of your visit devoted to testing and selecting among options will probably have a quite different feel relative to the rest of the visit and relative to more conventional applications of the visit tool. As stated earlier, to explore and to confirm are two very different activities.

Customer visits may sometimes play a minor supporting role in the evaluation of decision outcomes. Although in principle customer visits are just as ill-suited to measuring and tracking as to testing and selecting, visits can potentially supplement more formal and confirmatory approaches such as survey research. Thus, although it is important to confirm whether your customer satisfaction numbers have gone up or down, it is not always clear *why* the pattern of results takes the form it does. In this situation, a series of visits to customers whose satisfaction has increased and to customers whose satisfaction has not changed or has gotten worse is often illuminating. Such an application of customer visits serves as a reminder that the final stage of one decision cycle tends to merge with the first stage of the next decision cycle.

FOCUS GROUPS

In a focus group 8 to 12 consumers meet in a special facility for approximately two hours. The facility enables you to view the group from behind a one-way mirror and to make audio- and videotapes. The group discussion is moderated by a professional interviewer in accordance with objectives set by you. Focus groups are very similar to customer visits in their profile of suitable and unsuitable objectives, but somewhat more narrow in their applicability. The broader applicability of customer visits stems from its field research aspect (you go to the customer site) and the amount of time spent with individual customers.

Focus groups are simply a particular kind of interview, and this makes them useful in the initial exploratory stages of the decision cycle where you are scanning the environment and generating options. For instance, you might do some focus groups to identify emerging issues as viewed by customers within a particular segment of the market. At a later point, you might use focus groups to explore the pros and cons of several possible themes being considered for a new ad campaign. Part of generating options is defining these options in as much detail as possible, and the give-and-take of group interaction can be quite productive in this respect.

Focus groups are probably more effective at exploring, defining, and generating (stage two) than at identifying, describing, and monitoring (stage one); hence, their relegation to a contributing role during the environmental scanning stage. The power of focus groups comes from the interaction of customers within the group and whatever synergy results. The stimulus of group interaction is particularly useful when the goal is to generate fresh perspectives, define the differences among subgroups within the market, or explore consumer reactions. It is less useful when you want extensive descriptive data.

As with customer visits, generally speaking focus groups should never be used to select among options. The problem again centers on the small, bad samples of customers involved. Similarly, the skill brought by the outside interviewer to the conduct of focus groups is more than outweighed by the distorting potential of group influence and dominant participants. Problems of group influence and conformity pressure, together with the fact that focus groups are a laboratory rather than field procedure, make it impossible to recommend their use for even a contributing role during stage four, evaluation of outcomes. In this sense, focus groups constitute a more specialized tool than either secondary research or customer visits.

SURVEY RESEARCH

A survey takes place when a fixed set of questions is asked of a sample of customers. The sample is usually large and in many cases is carefully selected to represent the total population of customers. The comments that follow assume a telephone survey executed with a reasonably large and carefully selected sample in which the questions are largely *descriptive.*

Surveys can play a supporting role in environmental scanning. If you need a fairly exact factual description of the behaviors and simple perceptions of some customer group, and if such data cannot be gleaned from existing secondary research, then it may make sense to execute a survey. If, however, good secondary data already exist, it is rarely cost-effective to do your own survey, unless this takes the form of a small, fast, tailored survey directed at filling in a few gaps in the available secondary data. If the needed secondary data do not exist, and if you simply must have precise descriptive data on such matters as the frequency of certain applications among particular customer groups, or the average dollar amount of equipment purchases, or the average rating of your speed of response relative to key competitors, then a survey may make sense.

You should ask yourself, however, whether you really need precise descriptive data at this early point in the decision cycle. Is it really that important to be able to state with precision that 54% of the time this medical instrument will be used on auto accident victims, 24% on mothers undergoing childbirth, 18% on victims of gunshot wounds, and 4% with others? At this early point, what is the value added by these precise percentages, as opposed to what you could gain from a program of customer visits? A couple of dozen visits would probably reveal that auto accidents, childbirth, and gunshot wounds were "major" applications, even though the exact percentages would be unknown. In addition, and in contrast to the limited data supplied by a survey, the visits would provide opportunities to describe in depth how each of these applications place different demands on the instrument and on hospital staff, how this instrument interfaces with other equipment in the hospital, and so forth. Such rich descriptive data are often more useful, early in the decision cycle, than the thinner but more precise data yielded by surveys.

It is even more important to understand that surveys are far less useful in the generation of options than customer visits or focus groups. The relative weakness of surveys at this point in the decision cycle has several sources: (1) the fact that the questions to be asked are fixed in advance; (2) the reality that the phone interviewers who will implement the survey probably lack the ability, the motivation, or the opportunity to deeply probe customer answers; and (3) the unfortunate truth that the impersonal nature of the survey contact—the certain knowledge that one's responses are but grist for the statistical mill—will inhibit and limit the customer's investment of the energy required for discovery, exploration, and depth. Surveys are a confirmatory tool whose proper purpose is to limit, narrow, and specify; hence, this tool is largely incapable of expanding, broadening, and reconfiguring your understanding. Go easy on surveys early in the decision cycle.

Survey research comes into its own at the third stage of the decision cycle. All of the features that had been of dubious relevance or even liabilities at the earlier stages are here either neutralized or converted into strengths. In stage three the time for discovery and in-depth insight is past; now it is time to make hard choices and allocate limited resources. Perhaps you only have the resources to write new software for one or at most two of your instrument's applications, and you must determine which application predominates. Large investments may follow from decisions of this type, and it makes sense to invest a good sum of money in determining precisely which application is largest, or is growing the fastest, or has the weakest competitive presence.

Survey research is also of primary importance in the evaluation of outcomes. The classic example is the customer satisfaction surveys now conducted by many firms. These are usually telephone surveys, often conducted by a neutral outside firm, in which a standard series of questions is asked, focusing on product and vendor performance. The surveys are often repeated on a quarterly basis so that changes in satisfaction can be tracked over time. Another example is the tracking studies conducted after initiating an advertising campaign. These telephone surveys track awareness, brand attitude, and perceptions in those areas addressed by the advertising campaign. Here again, descriptive precision is an absolute requirement; otherwise, comparison over time becomes impossible.

CONJOINT ANALYSIS

In a conjoint study, consumers are presented with various product configurations, consisting of a set of features each delivered at a specified level. Thus, a computer monitor might be described in terms of resolution (1024 × 768 pixels or 1280 × 1024 pixels), price ($300, $400, or $500), screen size (15-inch, 17-inch, 19-inch), and so forth. Some subset of all the possible permutations is rated, and the mathematical analysis of these ratings gives insight into how consumers make trade-offs among different features and price points. Although there are many different ways to implement conjoint studies, regardless of format the goal is always to build a model of how a customer makes a choice among the various product offerings available, and thus to identify and quantify choice drivers (for example, how many dollars more, if any, will a consumer pay for a monitor with a resolution of 1280 × 1024?). The goal of conjoint analysis is thus to answer questions such as, Which product attributes drive the purchase decision? And how do customers make trade-offs between features and price?

Conjoint analysis is a valuable tool with strictly limited applicability. It makes little sense to use conjoint analysis during environmental scanning. Too little is known to justify use of a precise and narrowly focused tool of this kind. Conjoint analysis is not really appropriate for the generation of options either. This is because to perform conjoint analysis one must be able to say exactly what the key product attributes are, and part of the purpose of generating options is precisely to discover what product attributes might matter at all. Logically, environmental scanning and options generation precede and lay a foundation for more confirmatory techniques such as conjoint analysis.

The primary purpose of conjoint analysis is to assist in the selection of the best option, in the specific sense of the optimal product configuration. When serious uncertainty remains about whether one bundle of features or another is the most attractive to consumers, or about how to construct the optimal bundle of features, conjoint analysis is often a good choice. In turn, by the time one gets to the fourth and final stage of evaluating outcomes, the time for conjoint analysis may have passed.

EXPERIMENTS

In the simplest form of an experiment, you would administer two different treatments to two equivalent groups of customers and measure the response of each group to the treatment. The purpose of an experiment is to test which among a small number of treatments stimulates the greatest response. For example, you may be considering two different headlines for use in a direct mail pitch for some product or service, and you want to know which version will be most successful.

Like conjoint analysis, experiments are a narrowly applicable but extremely valuable tool. They are *not* of much use in the initial stages of environmental scanning and option generation or in the final stage of outcome evaluation. Early in the decision cycle you don't know enough to design a good experiment, whereas toward the end of the cycle you want market data, not experimental data. As was the case with conjoint analysis, experiments are primarily intended for use in option selection. In fact, their design corresponds exactly to the structure of many business decisions: that is, which of these options is the best? Moreover, experiments can sometimes answer a related and very important question: How *much* will we achieve? For instance, the response rate for the winning headline in the direct mail example would allow us to estimate what the response rate will be for the mass mailing, and this in turn allows us to draw up a pro forma income statement showing the cost of the promotion and the anticipated revenue gain.

Summary

Now that the contents of the market research toolbox have been spread out before you, and each tool briefly introduced and situated within the decision cycle, a few summary statements are in order.

1. Secondary research is *the* all-purpose market research tool. Partly because of the great diversity of the types of information that can

be obtained, and partly because much secondary research is both cheap and quickly obtainable, your first impulse in planning any inquiry into customers and markets should be to ask, Has somebody else already gathered the information I need?

2. Interviews and surveys are the most heavily used forms of primary research. The application of both these tools is a matter of asking questions and getting answers. If the issues with which you are concerned can be phrased as direct questions that customers are able to answer, then interviews or surveys will probably be rewarding.

3. Customer visits and focus groups anchor the exploratory end of the continuum. Here you may have some sense of what your key issues are, or what some of your questions may be, but you are uncertain about what kinds of answers are even possible. By contrast, surveys anchor the confirmatory end. Here you know both the key questions and the range of possible answers, and your goal is to pin down the exact frequency of each possible answer.

4. The selection of options, unlike the other decision stages, requires highly specialized research tools such as conjoint analysis and experimentation. It is an error and a mark of ignorance if the management of a firm exclusively conducts customer visits, or surveys, or a review of secondary resources when the primary goal is to select an option. Selecting the best option—pricing is a good example—often requires you to go beyond asking questions of customers and to instead create environments in which customers act or choose, so that you can analyze these behaviors to infer the answers you require. Both conjoint studies and experiments take this approach.

Do's and Don'ts

Do plan on using a variety of techniques over the course of a project. Make every effort to find the right tool for the job at hand. Every tool is specialized, and no tool is perfect.

Don't confuse exploratory and confirmatory techniques. Don't try to squeeze precision out of tools that can't provide it, and don't expect discoveries and new insights out of tools whose purpose is to narrow down the possibilities and eliminate options.

Don't fixate on specific research tools. Keep the focus on the decision to be made, and what information would be most helpful. Let the tool follow from the research objective.

References and Suggested Readings

Churchill, Gilbert A., and Dawn Iacobucci. 2001. *Marketing Research: Methodological Foundations,* 8th ed. Chicago: Southwestern.

Malhotra, Naresh. 2003. *Marketing Research: An Applied Orientation,* 4th ed. Upper Saddle River, NJ: Prentice Hall.

These are standard textbooks on marketing research that provide more detailed coverage of the specific tools discussed here and a thorough introduction to the statistical analysis of market research data.

Blankenship, A. B., George Edward Breen, and Allen Dutka. 1998. *State of the Art Marketing Research,* 2nd ed. New York: McGraw-Hill.

In this managerially focused textbook, the authors' extensive experience as practitioners shows in the detailed examples of how market research is applied to formulate and test business strategies.

Appendix 2A: Financial Planning for Market Research

An important part of planning for market research is estimating the budget required to fund the desired research. A simple equation is useful for laying out the conceptual issues involved in developing such a budget:

$$\text{Market Research Budget} = K \times R / F$$

Let K be the amount at stake with respect to the decision the research is intended to support. This amount is the contribution to profit that could be lost or foregone if the wrong decision is made (let contribution equal revenue minus the cost of goods sold, including fixed costs directly attributable to the decision, i.e., new capital equipment required to launch a new product). For instance, if upon introduction, crucial features in the product are lacking, what would that cost you? If you end up targeting the wrong application or the wrong group of customers, how expensive would this mistake be?

Second, let R be the reduction in the odds of making a wrong decision. This number is going to be quite a bit more fuzzy than the first number but can be estimated as follows. Suppose that 50% of new product introductions in your industry break even or turn a profit. The odds of failure (defined as incurring a loss) might then be estimated as 50%. You may then suppose that if effective market research were done, the odds of failure would decrease to 33%. R, the reduction in the odds of failure, is then estimated as 17%. Note that when the situation is terminally confusing, or when it is already quite clear, then R will be very small. In fact, R will be large only when candidates for the "right" decision can at least be glimpsed, *and* when there are a manageable number of such candidates, *and* when there is little confidence or consensus among decision makers about which candidate decision is the best one to make.

The underlying model here may be familiar to you from the decision-making and investment literatures. What we are doing here is estimating an expected return by quantifying an outcome and then weighting this quantity by its probability of occurrence. The logic may become more clear if we let K and R be vectors rather than simple quantities. In that event, K^1 through K^5 might correspond to the financial impact of (1) a disastrous new product introduction, (2) a disappointing new product introduction, (3) a mediocre product introduction, (4) a good but not great product introduction, and (5) a blockbuster success. R^1 would then be the reduction in odds of a disaster to be expected from conducting market research, R^2 would be the reduction in the odds of a disappointment, R^3 would be the reduction (or increase) in the odds of a mediocre result, R^4 the increase in the odds of a good result, and R^5 the increase in the odds of achieving a blockbuster success. Multiplying each element of K by the corresponding element of R, and summing over the products, would then yield the expected return from conducting market research.

F, the final element in the equation, might be thought of as a fudge factor. The result obtained from $K \times R$ reflects a chain of assumptions and guesses and will always be somewhat uncertain. It would be unfortunate if we invested $250,000 in market research, based on an expected return of $900,000, when in fact the possible return was only $200,000 or so. Letting F be a number like 5, 10, or even 20 makes it much more likely that the market research investment will return a multiple of itself—as opposed to more or less netting out to no gain. The analogy here is to value-based pricing. In this approach to pricing, if our offering is estimated to save the customer $200, we can't price it at $200, or $175, or even $125—a customer will not feel motivated to spend a certain $125 to *maybe* save $200. Only if we set a price on the order of $50, or $40, or even $20 will the customer be motivated to pay that certain amount to achieve savings that are only possible. The fudge factor serves the same purpose in the context of setting a maximum market research budget. If F is set at 5, then the market research investment has the potential to pay for itself five times over. This is appropriate, because there are other investments we could make to improve the odds of new product success (additional research and development [R&D], larger advertising budget, etc.), and many of these alternatives will at least be able to claim to pay back a multiple of themselves. The actual value of F in an individual case will vary with the conservatism of the firm and the perceived certainty of the estimate of $K \times R$.

The utility of the budget equation becomes apparent when it is combined with basic cost information concerning market research. These cost data will be discussed in more detail under the individual techniques, but some basic guidelines can be given. First, at the time of writing, $10,000 was about the floor for any execution of a particular market research technique (market intelligence can of course cost much less, and we will return to this point). A more common level of expenditure for an individual technique would be $20,000 to $30,000, and most projects of any magnitude will want to combine multiple research techniques. As a rule of thumb, then, a meaningful market research effort over the life of, say, a new product development project is unlikely to cost less than $50,000, will often exceed the $100,000 range, and may require much, much more.

With this cost information in hand we can put the financial planning equation to work. First, let the corporate contribution margin be 25%, let the reduction in the odds of failure attributable to good market research be 10%, and let the fudge factor be 20. With these numbers, we see that the new product has to have revenue potential of about $60,000,000 if one is to justify a market research budget on the order of $75,000. Specifically,

- If an important mistake in product design will cause the product to only break even rather than make a normal contribution to profit, the cost of a mistake (the amount at stake) is $15,000,000 (25% contribution × $60,000,000 in sales revenue).
- The maximum market research budget is then $1,500,000 (due to the expected 10% reduction in the odds of making a mistake).
- Applying the fudge factor of 20 yields the budget of $75,000.

By jiggering any of the assumptions just made, we can easily get the required revenue potential down to $20,000,000 or so. Thus, there exist software and other technology businesses with contribution margins well above 25% and even 50%. Alternatively, it may be more reasonable to assume that a mistaken product will produce an actual *loss* rather than break even. Moreover, the situation might be such that the reduction in the odds of error due to good market research will be more than 10%. Lastly, a more market-focused or more confident corporate culture might set a lower fudge factor. By a somewhat more heroic rearrangement of our assumptions (combining any two of the revisions just named) we could get the revenue level down to around $10,000,000. Even by the most heroic assumptions, $3 million to $5 million, in terms of product revenue, is probably the lower limit for justifying a sophisticated market research effort that includes at least two distinct data collection efforts and costs upward of $50,000.

Quite a number of useful conclusions emerge from this financial analysis. On the one hand, any Fortune 1000 corporation has many, many products with annual revenue potential in the tens of millions of dollars range, indicating again the pervasive opportunity for conducting market research. On the other, most small businesses and most technology start-ups will have to use ingenuity and rely heavily on intelligence gathering rather than on market research studies per se. In fact, it is probably fair to say that most mom-and-pop businesses cannot afford to purchase conventional market research. Much can be done on a shoestring, but it will mostly consist of marketing intelligence, secondary data, and a simple kind of customer visit.

Continuing along these lines, the higher the profit margin, the greater the opportunity to do market research (or make any other investment in long-term market success). Conversely, the lower the capital costs for introducing and then terminating a failed new product, the less the justifiable expenditure on market research. When I began consulting for insurance and financial services firms, I was quite struck by the contrast between their research budgeting and that of the equipment manufacturers with which I was most familiar. To design and manufacture a new instrument or other electronic product inevitably entails a substantial R&D and capital expenditure. Introducing a new financial service or program often incurs modest costs that are several orders of magnitude less. In such cases, actual market introduction provides a relatively quick and inexpensive test of whether the program was or was not a good idea. Given this low cost of test-by-launch, upfront market research has to be inexpensive if it is to be done at all. The moral of the story: if it won't cost you much to be wrong, you shouldn't spend very much on market research.

The logic of the equation has particularly troubling implications for program managers. This job category includes people who manage documentation, customer service, or lines of product accessories and the like. Program managers have no less need for market and customer information than project and product managers (these are parallel job titles in the engineering and marketing functions), but their efforts seldom have the kind of assignable revenue impact required to justify a substantial market research budget. Two solutions make sense for people in the program manager position. The first is to concentrate on intelligence gathering, and the second is to find ways to piggyback on the market research efforts of project and product managers. If a program manager can add a question or two to a research study, this may have little effect on the cost of the study while yielding an invaluable supplement to his or her ongoing intelligence effort. Program managers who regularly execute such piggyback strategies gain a constant stream of research data at little direct cost.

On a final note, a more subtle implication of the financial equation is that a short-term focus makes it difficult to adequately budget for market research. For technology companies in particular, substantial market research efforts may be best focused at the *product platform* level and not at the level of an individual product configuration. That is, just as home stereo manufacturers offer a variety of amplifier power and quality levels, so also many technology products come in large and small, high-end and low-end versions, each aimed at a particular application or industry segment. Although each is a somewhat different product, all rest on the same basic assembly of technologies—the platform. Sales at the platform level, especially over the several years' life of the platform, will almost always be large enough to justify a substantial research budget (although product life cycles have often shrunk to months, platform life cycles still last for years). Unfortunately, accounting systems and organizational groupings are often structured in terms of products. If the platform has no budget code, and if no team or individual has platform responsibility, then effective budgeting for market research becomes difficult.

Stepping back, the financial equation provides a way of acting on the truism that market research has to be considered an investment. It becomes clear that market research really *is* expensive, and that the stakes have to be high to justify it. Conversely, the equation serves as a lever for use with those penny-wise, pound-foolish technical managers who choke at the idea of spending $50,000 on something as intangible and squishy as market research. When a new product line is expected to generate revenue on the order of $100 million, and there are some excruciating uncertainties concerning its design and intended audience, then a market research expenditure of $100,000 is a trivial price to pay if the odds of success can be materially improved. Note again that this kind of high-stakes situation is most likely to arise at the level of a product line or product platform, and is much less common at the level of an individual product configuration or stock-keeping unit.

Note also that while the *K* component in the equation provides a bracing reminder that market research planning is basically about money, the *R* component provides an equally important reminder that market research itself really boils down to uncertainty reduction. To the extent that you feel certain about what will happen or what will work, market research grows less necessary. For instance, if management has already made up its mind (for good or bad reasons), then market research can't reduce the odds of a wrong decision because it is not going to have *any* effect on the decision. Studies conducted under these circumstances are just politics and basically a waste of time and money. Conversely, when uncertainty is very high—your environment is essentially chaotic—market research may be beside the point. Since this situation is the more common one in technology firms, an example might help. Suppose that the success or failure of a given project hinges entirely on whether the technical standard to which it adheres does or does not end up dominating the market some years hence. Suppose further that the dominance or defeat of that technical standard is not within the control of company management or of any definable group of people, that it will, in fact, be a function of so many interlocking factors that it is impossible to grasp them all or depict their interrelations. In that situation, the most that market research may be able to offer is an early warning of whether the technical standard is or is not moving toward dominance. If that early warning would not be helpful, then it may be best to spend nothing at all on market research in this connection, and put the money to other uses, such as lobbying for the chosen standard at technical gatherings.

Perhaps you expected more than "uncertainty reduction" from market research. You hoped, in a nutshell, to achieve some kind of *guarantee* of making the right decision. Not to be too blunt, you are naive. Market research is a social science, not a physical science, and a young social science at that. It can reduce uncertainty but never eliminate it. On average, across a large business, over a period of years, this small reduction in uncertainty can be very lucrative and repay the cost of the research many times over. But all market research can ever do is reduce the odds of making a costly error and increase the odds of making a profitable decision. If instead it is certainty that you want, then I suggest you go to a chapel.

PART II

3

Secondary Research

S econdary market research refers to any data gathered for one purpose by one party and then put to a second use by or made to serve
the purpose of a second party. Secondary market research is thus the
broadest and most diffuse tool within the toolbox, because it includes
virtually any information that can be reused within a market research
context. Secondary research is also the closest thing to an all-purpose
market research tool, because virtually every project makes some use of
secondary data and almost any decision stage may incorporate some
kind of secondary research. As a general rule, relatively speaking
secondary research also is the cheapest and quickest form of market
research. You ignore or skimp on it at your peril. Its range of application is limited only by your ingenuity.

It is helpful to distinguish between internal and external secondary
research. Internal secondary data consist of information gathered elsewhere within your firm. The major categories include (1) sales reports,
(2) customer databases, and (3) reports from past primary market
research. Sales reports generally give data broken down by product category, region, and time period. More sophisticated systems also give
breakdowns by distribution channel, level of price discount, customer
type (large, medium, small), and similar categories. Customer databases
might include a recording of brief descriptive data on all accounts
(industry, contact person, phone number, purchase history); a log of
tech support or response center calls; a record of specific products purchased; and the like. Records of past primary market research include
results of surveys and focus groups conducted in prior years, accumulated customer visit trip reports, and so forth.

External secondary research includes (1) information gathered by government agencies such as the Census Bureau, (2) information compiled for sale by commercial vendors, and (3) various kinds of public and quasi-public information available from diverse sources. Government agencies collect an enormous amount of demographic (e.g., the Census Bureau) and economic trend data (e.g., federal and state departments of commerce). In recent years the United States government has also done more to help companies seeking to export by providing information on overseas markets. Entire volumes are devoted to simply listing and cross-referencing various government reports.

An important kind of secondary data available from commercial vendors is known as the syndicated report. For a syndicated report an analyst compiles a variety of data, using libraries, databases, phone calls, and even some primary market research such as interviews or surveys, in order to address a topic such as trends in the in-home computer networking market, 2005–2008. The goal is to sell the report to as many network equipment companies as can be persuaded to buy. Syndicated reports may be one-time efforts or may appear periodically. Because the appetite for data is so huge, especially in technology markets, a whole industry of syndicated report vendors has grown up to satisfy this appetite. These commercial vendors function as one part librarian, one part statistician, one part detective, and one part proxy market researcher. They employ analysts who are in the business of being industry experts, and a certain number of hours of these analysts' time can be purchased along with the vendor's reports.

Public and quasi-public data sources include anything published in a magazine or newspaper. Most industries have a few trade magazines devoted to coverage of companies, events, and trends. A few industries, like the computer and telecommunications industries, are the focus of a slew of publications. Similarly, most industries of note are, on occasion, the subject of a feature article in the *Wall Street Journal, New York Times, Los Angeles Times,* or other respected newspaper. Trade associations, university survey research centers, nonprofit agencies, and others publish data from time to time. With the spread of computerized information retrieval services (everything from the traditional Dialog to the Web) it has become easier to bring together data from a wide range of sources and publications.

Procedure

Three types of procedure are relevant here: steps to be taken at the firm level, to facilitate the collection and use of secondary research throughout the firm; steps to be taken by individuals within a firm in connection with either a *market research project* or as part of *ongoing market intelligence* efforts. The logic of the first distinction is that an individual contributor or manager will find it difficult to do excellent secondary research unless an infrastructure has already been put in place at the firm level. The logic of the second distinction is based on the difference between a market research study and ongoing market intelligence gathering, as set out in Chapter 1, and the differing demands these place on secondary research. A discipline common to almost all uses of secondary data is search, and Appendix 3A addresses search strategies.

STEPS TO BE TAKEN BY THE FIRM

1. *Upgrade the corporate library.* Although major corporations have had internal libraries for many years, of late the demands on and the potential benefits from these libraries have rapidly escalated. Today in the marketing area the primary holding is not books or even periodicals but the syndicated reports bought from various vendors. Because so many individuals have a use for particular reports on occasion, most corporations of any size centralize the purchase of market research reports, and have the collection maintained by either a division of the library or a department within the market research area.

A carefully thought out strategy of which reports to buy from which vendors is a must. It may be quite difficult for an individual project manager to get the funds or find the time to locate a valuable report that is not part of the collection—if he or she even learns of its existence at all. Hence, the best way to promote the use of secondary data is to arrange to have on hand most of the most useful reports.

A good library has an effective indexing and cataloging strategy so that relevant data can be easily located. A good library will also be on the lookout for specialized resources—services that compile statistics, bulletins that bring together articles from a variety of trade publications, and so forth. Finally, a good library keeps up with new technology for collecting and distributing information, such as electronic clipping services, wherein a semi-intelligent agent searches for articles meeting a profile set up by a user. Phrases like the Information Society and the Data Explosion are not hype when it comes to secondary data. It's a full-time job keeping up with the proliferation of sources of secondary data, and successful firms hire librarians or outsource to consultants who can do this.

2. *Provide appropriate consultation services.* Whether located in the market research area or the corporate library, one or more persons have to serve as reference librarians who can proactively help a manager find relevant resources rather than simply responding to queries. Inasmuch as most market research vendors provide several hours of their analysts' time when reports are purchased, the reference librarian is also the logical choice to serve as gatekeeper to these analysts. Without a gatekeeper, the few hours of analyst time may be frittered away. Lastly, whether in-house or outsourced, the library should make available a professional database searcher—someone who can quickly devise and execute effective search strategies of electronic databases.

Bring the Library to the Desktop

Because more and more information is available in electronic form, and because information in hard-copy form is in any case a problem for multinational and decentralized firms, in the future most if not all of the corporate library will have to be made accessible from the desktop computer of the individual user. Most major firms had already made substantial progress toward this goal by the mid-1990s.

An important part of desktop access is proactive posting of information by the library to the individual user. Generally, users sign up for certain E-mail aliases (i.e., they put themselves on the distribution list for certain kinds of E-mail) and the library regularly pumps out the appropriate information to the various aliases. This might include recent library acquisitions, types of bulletins now available, and so on.

EVALUATE SOURCES OF INFORMATION

Quality can vary dramatically across vendors, and also within vendors depending on particular areas of expertise. It behooves any substantial purchaser of these reports to periodically evaluate the strengths and weaknesses of each research vendor based on past experience, and to make these evaluations available for consultation by project, product, and program managers.

STEPS TO BE TAKEN FOR A MARKET RESEARCH PROJECT

Identify Relevant Library Holdings

Early in the environment scanning stage you should budget some time for reading and browsing in the library. For example, you may try to construct graphs of trends in sales or market share by assembling a series of syndicated reports. For a second example, reading a set of reports interpreting industry events will help to constellate key issues in your mind.

Assemble Relevant Internal Secondary Data

Using data from within your firm, you may be able to produce illuminating breakdowns of where sales performance has been strong or weak, profiles of typical customer applications, segmentation analyses of your customer base, tabulations of reported problems and complaints, and so forth. If you can assemble past primary market research reports that address, however tangentially, your area of concern, then you may gain perspective beyond what you obtained from reading outside analysts' discussions.

Decide on a Search Strategy

If the scope of your project justifies it, you may want to mount a search of databases, or sign up for a consultation with some market research analyst. You would go this route, for instance, if you were a product manager charged with preparing a backgrounder or white paper on whether the firm should expand into a particular market or pursue product development in a specific direction. In such instances, your responsibility is to pull together all the information available on this topic, and an effortful search strategy can be justified.

Decide Whether to Supplement the Available Secondary Data with Primary Market Research

Sometimes you will learn everything you need to know from secondary data; or more exactly, you will learn enough from secondary data that it would not be cost-effective to conduct additional primary market research. If you do decide to collect primary data, as you probably will in many cases, your definition of the problem and your research objectives will be much improved by your secondary research.

STEPS TO BE TAKEN FOR ONGOING MARKET INTELLIGENCE GATHERING

Make a Commitment

Assume that you have a forward-looking corporate library as described above. The question becomes how to take best advantage of the ocean of available information that floods in on a weekly basis. You're not a librarian and neither are you an analyst who has the luxury of studying an industry or topic full-time. At most you can devote a few hours a week to library-based market intelligence gathering. And that's really the first step: to commit a certain period of time—something you can reasonably hope to achieve in all but the busiest week—to finding and reading materials that will add to your stock of marketing intelligence.

Sign Up for the Appropriate Newsfeeds, Bulletins, and E-Mail Aliases

Be familiar with the materials that can be sent to your desktop. Flag articles that look interesting and read them. It helps a lot if there are certain times in your week when this kind of reading is easy rather than hard to do. Setting up good habits is half the battle.

Develop a Personal Clipping Service or Search Profile

This has gotten easier of late, but it remains an innovation and may or may not be possible at your firm. What you want is a set of keywords, or some more complicated search routine, that can be run against a database on a periodic basis (once a month or once a quarter). Here are some examples that would be relevant for a typical product manager: (1) mention of either of your two largest competitors or their important brands in any of several leading periodicals; (2) mention of the words "new" or "introduce" in conjunction with the name of your product category; (3) mention of any of the several major applications for your product (it will take practice to specify this search tightly enough); or (4) mention of the words "trend" with "market share," "sales," or "profit" in conjunction with your industry or product category. This kind of search tends to yield articles that you really want to read, and receiving such highly relevant articles in turn reinforces the habit of making regular forays for market intelligence.

Build Mental Models of Your Markets

I would imagine that almost every product, project, and program manager already engages in a fair amount of reading. The point to remember is that you will read with greater understanding and enhanced recall if you *read actively*—meaning that you read with reference to mental models that you are trying to build, test, modify, or rebut. A manager once remarked to me that he thought the real shortcoming of American managers was that they did not put enough energy into constructing conceptual models of the driving forces and key factors within their industry. I have no way of proving or disproving this criticism. I do know that your reading will be more rewarding if it is done with reference to mental models you have built and modified over time.

In the market intelligence mode, it is best to keep these models simple and basic. I have in mind core statements that reflect what you think you know. Here are some examples in generic form.

1. Competitor X's biggest advantage is . . . Its biggest shortcoming is . . .

2. Customers of type Y place the greatest importance on . . .

3. There are Z major types of customers in this market. They are distinguished by . . .

4. Our major strengths in the marketplace are . . . Our significant weaknesses are . . .

5. Decision A was successful because . . . Decision B failed because . . .

Of course, the reality of professional life is that the activity of just reading is the kind of activity that inevitably drops toward the bottom of your to-do list. Searching for information that refines, deepens, or extends your model of what's really going on may yield the motivation needed to persevere.

Examples

Because of the diversity of secondary research, some typical applications will be given in place of specific examples.

Sales and market share analysis. Analysts compile data and do detective work to estimate market shares of key competitors, including breakdowns by application, by product subcategory, by region, by customer industry, and so forth. As part of this analysis, sales trends, including growth rates, are discussed.

Trend analysis. Often the goal of a report is to go beyond collecting and reporting specific numbers to encompass interpretation and analysis of underlying dynamics, critical success factors, implications of recent events and decisions, and the like.

Customer segmentation. Reports may suggest a variety of schema for distinguishing and grouping various types of customers, and discuss the particular needs and requirements of each segment.

Competitor analysis. Reports may dissect and critique business and marketing strategies of key competitors. Analyses will indicate strengths and weaknesses of products, and describe markets where each competitor enjoys advantages or suffers disadvantages.

Strengths and Weaknesses

An important strength of secondary research is that it is generally quickly available for a modest cost. This is no small advantage in many business situations. Moreover, as discussed earlier, it is difficult to do any kind of primary market research for less than $10,000. If a few days in the library can remove most of the key uncertainties about market facts, albeit without giving exact answers to all one's questions, this may save you tens of thousands of dollars. The key fact about secondary research, then, is that it already exists and is readily available. At a minimum, it can improve the focus of any primary research you do choose to conduct.

A particular advantage of *internal* secondary data is that it uses categories and breakdowns that reflect a corporation's preferred way of structuring the world. Outside analysts may use very different and not always comparable breakdowns. Internal databases often contain very specific and detailed information, and very fine-grained breakdowns. Finally, one can generally get a fairly good idea of the validity of the data because one can discuss how it was gathered with the people responsible.

A particular strength of *external* secondary data is the objectivity of the outside perspective it provides. These reports are written by analysts with broad industry experience not beholden to any specific product vendor. Whereas product managers have many responsibilities, and may be new to their position, analysts spend all of their time focusing on market trends or industry analysis.

A final advantage of specific instances of secondary data is that these may be the *only* available source of specific pieces of information. This is often true of government data, for instance. It would be impossible (and foolish) for any individual firm to attempt to match the efforts of the U.S. Census Bureau or Department of Commerce.

The most important weakness of secondary data stems from the fact that these data were gathered by other people for other purposes. Hence, often it does not exactly address your key question of concern. The answers, although not irrelevant, lack specificity, use breakdowns that are not comparable to other data, or don't address key issues in enough depth or from the desired perspective. Sometimes this potential limitation is not a factor, as in cases where the information you want is exactly the kind that secondary research is best suited to answer (e.g., aggregate market data). In other cases, particularly when customer requirements are a focal concern, or when insight into the psychology and motivation of buying is crucial, secondary data may only scratch the surface.

Some external secondary data may be of suspect quality. One should never fall into the trap of assuming that a report, simply because it is well written and associated with a recognized consulting firm, offers some kind of window onto absolute truth. Quality varies—by analyst, by firm, by type of information, and by market category. Reports are prepared by people. These people may be very intelligent or less so, meticulous or sloppy, thorough or slapdash, well informed or beset by unexamined assumptions. Most large buyers of secondary data develop a sense for which consulting firms are strong (or weak) in a particular area. This judgment may be explicit in documents prepared by corporate staff, or implicit and locked in the heads of employees who work with these vendors on a regular basis. It behooves you to tap into this collective wisdom before spending large amounts of money or basing crucial decisions on a consulting firm's data. In general, when reviewing a report you have to carefully examine the appendix describing study methodology, and come to your own judgment about study quality. If there is no methodology section to examine, or if the sampling procedure is never explained, then beware!

A weakness characteristic of internal secondary data such as sales reports and customer databases is that they describe only your *existing* customers. Do not assume that these data can be extrapolated to describe the market as a whole. Rather, there is every reason to believe that your customers do not exactly reproduce the characteristics of the total market.

Be careful of data that may be dated or too old. Technology markets often change rapidly. Lastly, be aware that secondary data are less likely to exist outside the United States. Particularly in Asia and in developing countries, the secondary data that you'd like to have and could reasonably expect to find in the United States or Europe may simply not exist.

Do's and Don'ts

Do ask your colleagues' opinions of specific vendors' performance.

Don't take numbers in syndicated reports at face value. Read the appendix and consider the methodology used. Pay particular attention to how samples were gathered and always maintain a healthy skepticism.

Do triangulate across vendors. Compare numbers gathered from different sources by different methods. Often the truth lies somewhere in between.

Don't try to absorb a mass of secondary data all at once. Develop habits of regular reading; keep a notebook devoted to insights, reminders, and mental notes about possible models.

Suggested Readings

Patzer, Gordon L. 1995. *Using Secondary Data in Marketing Research: United States and Worldwide.* Westport, CT: Quorum Books.

Stewart, David, and Michael Kamins. 1992. *Secondary Research: Information Sources and Methods,* 2nd ed. Newbury Park, CA: Sage.

Both of these books provide a comprehensive guide to choosing and using secondary research. Stewart has more extensive examples of the strategic use of this information, whereas Patzer adds an international focus.

2004 Greenbook. 2004. New York: American Marketing Association, New York Chapter.

The most comprehensive guide to market research suppliers and service providers, updated annually.

Finally, all market research textbooks have a discussion of secondary research (e.g., the Churchill and Malhotra volumes listed at the end of Chapter 2), and the most recent edition can be consulted for up to-date lists of data sources.

Appendix 3A: Search Techniques for Gathering Marketing Intelligence

Today no person can claim to be skilled in the conduct of secondary research if he or she is lacking in search skills. The proliferation of electronic databases of all kinds, the explosion of data on the Web, and the availability of search engines such as Google make it imperative that you acquire good search skills. Searching is a skill, and this section discusses just a few of the basics in the context of doing market research. At the time this book was revised (2004), the marketplace for search engines and services was very dynamic. Hence, the focus is not on specific resources (which may become obsolete) but on fundamental strategies that should stand the test of time.

> Principle 1: Not all data are electronic.
>
> Corollary 1a: Electronic data available at your desktop are not always the most tractable source of the information you need.

I suppose there may come a time when all secondary data of any note will exist in sharable electronic form, but that time is not yet. The older the information, the less likely it is to be found in electronic form (and compiling trend data often requires older information). Even in 2004, some reasonable proportion of the typesetting and printing technologies used to publish commercial market research data continue to make use of proprietary data formats that cannot be made to produce sharable electronic data without additional time or effort. Under these circumstances, the more voluminous the data, and the more specialized, the less likely it is to exist outside its native paper format. Hence, it will often be timely and cost-effective to search a library catalogue for physical resources early in your search.

The corollary is that even when all the information you seek is available in electronic form, and accessible at your desktop, this may still not be the best way to access the data. Most electronic retrieval systems use the monitor screen (the amount of info that fits on a screen) as the unit of presentation, so that they only show 10 links at a time, or one page of data, and so forth. Accessing the next page of links or the next page of data involves a delay that can be substantial. (Yes, broadband Internet access can be fast, but how often does *your* broadband connection live up to its maximum potential of near-instantaneous screen replacement?) The fact is, flipping paper pages can be much faster than refreshing page access on a computer screen. The advantage of perusing a paper volume (assuming it has a table of contents and an index and makes good use of headings and titles instead of searching an electronic version on screen) can be substantial. The advantage of paper is greatest when you undertake a fuzzy search (i.e., when you can recognize useful data when you see it, but can't necessarily formulate the object of your search in any precise way).

The first principle of search, then, is that paper can be searched too, and that searches of paper sources can sometimes be more effective than searches of electronic data. Don't fall prey to the silliness (a lingering remnant of the dot.com boom time) that treats information-on-paper as some kind of medieval entrapment to be avoided at all cost.

Principle 2: Not all electronic data are freely accessible via the Web.

Corollary 2a: Search specialized sites, not just Google.

Although more and more data are stored in electronic form, the owner of the data does not always make it publicly available. A typical example is the archives of past issues that print publishers maintain. Here the data are stored in electronic form, and are searchable, but these data are not searchable from Google or any other search engine. These data can only be searched from within the publisher's site. The cover page or entry point to the private database may be located through a search engine, but the actual contents cannot be searched by means of the search engine—the spider or other program used by the search engine was never allowed to index the contents of the database. There are all kinds of reasons why private databases will continue to exist walled off from Web search engines. The owner may wish to charge a fee for access (as in the case of the print publication's archives), security considerations may make it undesirable to allow indexing of the database, data format issues may make this difficult, and so forth.

The practical implication is that when you are searching for a particular kind of specialized information, Google (or any other Web search engine) may not be your best bet. Instead, you need to locate the appropriate specialized database that can then be searched. Sometimes Google can tip you off to the existence of a specialized database; sometimes you can ask a librarian; and sometimes, this knowledge is something you acquire by experience.

An example may be useful. Suppose you want to find the consumer magazines with the highest circulation among males. Put another way, you are looking for the most cost-effective way to reach millions of male magazine readers and want a list of likely magazines for further investigation into costs, and so forth. If you had followed principle 1, then your librarian might have directed you to one of the paper volumes published by *Adweek* or SRDS, which would contain such a list. If you were new to media planning and unaware that such compilations of circulation data have been published in print for many years, then you might attempt a Google search. Let's see how that might play out.

The first question is, What search string should you use? Some possibilities might include the following:

1. "Which magazines have the most male readers?"
2. "Magazine circulation male female 2004"
3. "Magazine circulation data"
4. "Magazine circulation"

The first string might be characterized as a natural language query—you phrase the search string just as you would ask the question of an expert if one were available. However, when attempted in summer 2004 on Google, this string failed to produce any useful links on the first page. Although search technology is moving toward being able to handle natural language queries, in this case Google throws up sites that have one word ("magazine") or another ("male"), but there don't appear to be many sites that have all these words, and none of the top links was relevant.

Now consider the second search string. You might have said to yourself, what I'm really looking for is a table of some kind—let's search on the sort of headings that such a table would have. Unfortunately, what this string turns up is circulation data for individual magazines; the top links do not yield a site comparing multiple magazines.

When you don't succeed with your first one or two attempts, it is generally a good idea to rephrase your query a couple of times, using different rules. As an example of a rule, if you started with a long search string, simplify it; if you started with a simple string, add some more keywords. Since we started with longer strings, the next attempt might be the third example: "magazine circulation data." Unfortunately, this string also tends to throw up the Web sites of individual magazines reporting their own data.

Finally, the simplest possible relevant string would appear to be the fourth example: "magazine circulation." In July 2004, that proved to be the optimal search string—the topmost link leads to the web site of *Advertising Age,* one of the leading publishers of data on magazines and other media. A quick navigation through the *Ad Age* site takes one to the data center, where one of the tables lists the top consumer magazines with male and female readership data broken out.

> Principle 3: Small changes in search string vocabulary can have a huge impact on which sites rise to the top of a search engine's rankings.

> Principle 4: The optimal search string—specific or general, long or short, natural language or keywords—is seldom a priori obvious. Be prepared to systematically vary the structure of your search string.

In the example we looked only at the first page of links. Sometimes I look at a second and third page if I am enamored of my search string. Generally speaking, though, I would vary the search string a couple of times before delving too deeply into the second, third, or fourth page of links. If several search strings haven't produced the desired result, then I might repeat the most promising and look at a second, third, or fourth page of links (it rarely pays to go much further).

It didn't happen on this search, but sometimes a Google search will take you right to the desired site on the first try, whereupon you will discover that that site has the desired information—but you have to pay for it. (This would have happened if Google had pulled up the *Adweek* site, another advertising trade magazine with a great deal of data, much of which is not free.) In that event, might there be another site that has most of what you want, for free? Sometimes there is, and sometimes there isn't. It is naive to expect that valuable information will always be free simply because you located it on the Web.

Finally, sometimes the search process succeeds, but is much more laborious than in the example. Thus, you try several search strings without much luck; go back to a string and review the second and third page of links; explore several of these links, each of which turns out to be a dead end; try another string, which does produce an interesting site, which doesn't have what you want, but gives you an idea for a different search string or a different source to consult; which finally yields the information you seek. That is the nature of the search today.

Summary: Search Strategy for Secondary Research

1. Ask a librarian (or review your own experience) to see if an appropriate print reference exists. (The quickest way to solve the example question would have been to open *Adweek's Guide to Media,* consult the table of contents, and open the book to the desired table. If you routinely worked with media data, some such book would have been on your shelf.)

2. If no printed reference work exists, inquire as to whether there are relevant trade magazines that might be expected to publish these data. If so, search first on their Web sites. (Again, information stored in a database may not be accessible from the public Web—you only detect it if you get to the Web site and use that Web site's own search function.)

3. If steps 1 and 2 fail, attempt a search of the Web using Google or a similar engine. Here, type the first reasonable query that pops into your head. (It is surprising how often this is successful.) If at first you don't succeed, try the following strategies, in roughly this order: (a) vary the search string; (b) look at second, third, and fourth pages of links; (c) take the best links and see where they lead; (d) try a meta-search engine or a directory like Yahoo; and last, (e) sleep on it. A different and better search string is most likely to occur to you if you step away from the problem for a while.

4

Customer Visits

In a customer visit one or more decision makers from a vendor directly interacts with one or more customers or potential customers of that vendor. Of course, salespeople and customer support personnel have such contacts daily with customers. For our purposes, however, a customer visit, considered as a kind of marketing intelligence or market research, specifically occurs when a decision maker from outside these areas interacts with customers. For example, research and development would not normally be considered a customer contact function. Hence, when an engineer travels to a customer site, that is a customer visit. So also when a product marketer as opposed to a member of the field sales organization makes a presentation to customers, or when a member of general management or someone in manufacturing or someone in quality control travels to the customer site.

Note that the term *decision maker* is intended to be very general. It refers to anyone (not just upper management) who makes any kind of decision that affects customers. Thus, in new product development, design engineers are decision makers; in total quality efforts, manufacturing engineers and quality staff members are decision makers; in the design of marketing programs, marketing staff members are decision makers; and so forth. The term *customer* is intended to be similarly inclusive, and encompasses present and potential customers, competitors' customers, internal-to-the-vendor customers, and key opinion leaders or influential persons who may shape customer buying decisions. Similarly, the individuals at customer firms who may participate in customer visits are not limited to purchasing agents, general management, or other traditional "vendor contact" positions, but may include anyone who is involved in the consideration, buying, installation, maintenance, use, or disposal of the vendor's product.

Customer visits may be distinguished as *outbound*—where the vendor travels to the customer—or *inbound*—where the customer travels to the vendor site. Although we will focus on outbound visits to the work site that involve face-to-face contact, face-to-face contacts may also occur at neutral sites such as trade shows.

We can further distinguish *ad hoc* from *programmatic* customer visits. An ad hoc visit is any contact where marketing research is *not* the primary agenda or driving force behind the visit, but simply one of several motives. By contrast, a customer visit program consists of a series of visits that are conducted precisely to achieve some market research objective, and for which market research is the primary and often the sole agenda. Be aware that while ad hoc visits provide an important opportunity for marketing intelligence gathering, programmatic visits can be considered a market research technique just like focus groups, surveys, and experiments. Because the procedures are quite different in the two cases, ad hoc and programmatic visits are discussed separately.

Ad Hoc Visits for Marketing Intelligence

A truly astonishing number of ad hoc contacts with customers already occur. Engineers go on troubleshooting visits; product marketers give presentations explaining corporate strategy; managers make visits to support salespeople who are trying to close deals; customers come to the vendor for tours; both parties meet at trade shows; and so forth. When I poll a group of a dozen managers on the number of such visits they and their direct reports will likely make next quarter, the number generally exceeds 100. What makes these visits "ad hoc" is that the primary agenda is to fix, to tell, or to sell, and not to learn. Moreover, at most firms today these visits are planned and executed in isolation from one another. Each person conducts his or her own visits as the need arises, one by one, without coordination across individuals or over time.

Even more astonishing than the number and diversity of these ad hoc visits is the fact that most firms do little to harvest marketing intelligence from them. For very little out-of-pocket cost, ad hoc visits could become a valuable source of insight into customer concerns, customer perspectives, and emerging market trends. Best of all, the effort to harness ad hoc visits would allow you to deliver customer and market information directly to a wide range of decision makers across functional areas in the organization. Five steps are required to achieve these benefits:

1. *Resolve to change.* The present haphazard approach to nonprogrammatic visits evolved naturally over time in your organization. There is no reason to expect it to change overnight or without effort. For these visits to become an adjunct to marketing intelligence efforts, a manager or managers must commit to a change in habit, and this change in habit must be coordinated and sustained over time.

It is probably best to start small, at the business team or business unit level, or in some portion of a division. Call a meeting of the relevant players. Discuss the value of taking steps to move closer to customers. Lastly—and it is this step that takes you beyond good intentions to an actionable plan—generate and agree upon two or three perennial questions that everyone commits to asking during each ad hoc customer visit that occurs over the next quarter.

2. *Articulate perennial questions.* A perennial question is a general, discussion-starting query that can be asked of any customer with whom you happen to have 10 minutes. Here are some examples:

1. Why did you select our product?
2. What's the worst difficulty you have in working with us?
3. What business problems are causing you to lose sleep?
4. How do you compare us with our competitors? What are our strengths and weaknesses?

Of course, you don't have to use any one of these examples. What you must do is come up with questions of this type that reflect your particular marketing intelligence needs of the moment. A good perennial question starts a discussion, opens avenues for exploration, and provides an opportunity to probe for details and clarification. A wide range of such questions may prove suitable from time to time. The important thing is that everyone commit to asking these questions at every opportunity.

3. *Log customer profiles.* If the articulation of perennial questions converts good intentions to action, it is the development of customer profiles that sustains that action. If you do not find some way to capture and record the results of asking perennial questions, then you have taken only a small step toward mastering the potential of ad hoc visits. With perennial questions alone, learning improves but retention may not, and sharing of learning is much less likely to occur.

The solution is to log the results of ad hoc visits in the form of a profile. This consists of a very brief document prepared immediately after the visit (brevity is important—multiplying onerous paperwork requirements is not the way to succeed in today's business environment). The first part of the profile should be some kind of "header page" containing information of the sort normally maintained in customer databases: annual purchase volume, type of application, product configuration, and the like. The heart of the profile consists of the gist of the answers given by this customer to the perennial questions asked. Also important is the visitor's takeaway—any insights or impressions triggered by this visit. In sum, the profile documents the learning that occurred as a result of this visit.

4. *Review profiles.* Thus far we have added coordination (agreed-upon perennial questions) and capture (logged profiles) to what had been thoroughly ad hoc visits. The next step is to promote sharing and discussion, so that insights do not remain locked in the heads of individuals. A good way to do this is to call a meeting, after several months have elapsed, of all the people who committed to asking perennial questions. Prior to that meeting, make hard copies of all the profiles thus far accumulated and distribute them to all participants. Request that everyone read everyone else's profiles as preparation for the meeting. What happens now is that for the first time you see what other people have been hearing from customers. One customer, answering one question, constitutes a very weak data point; but now for the first time we have 20, 30, or 50 customers, all of whom have been asked the same question. You may discover that an answer you received but thought was unusual or an exceptional case has in fact cropped up in several other profiles. Conclusion: something is happening in the marketplace.

The purpose of this review meeting, then, is to compare notes, to reflect upon patterns, trends, and puzzles, and in general to answer the question, What are our customers trying to tell us? Out of the meeting will come understanding, a shared vision, and action plans. Not least, the meeting should consider whether the same or different perennial questions should be used going forward.

5. *Database visits and profiles.* The final step is to store a record of visits and profiles in some kind of database. Even a simple record of who visited whom and when would be invaluable in planning future ad hoc and programmatic visits. With such a record, anyone contemplating a customer visit could easily discover when this customer was last visited, who did the visit, and what issues emerged. Similarly, as more and more profiles accumulate, it becomes possible to do more interesting analyses of customer issues. Text retrieval software allows a marketing strategist to search for any mention of competitor X, or a design engineer to search for any mention of functionality Y or application Z. Moreover, managers planning programmatic customer visits can review profiles to determine likely candidates for inclusion.

Summary. Better coordination of ongoing ad hoc customer visits costs very little money and promises a wealth of data on customer perceptions, feelings, and reactions. In contrast, most other forms of marketing intelligence emphasize more quantitative and factual kinds of data. There is also a secondary benefit of adding a learning objective to these visits. Customers are most accustomed to vendors whose primary mode of self-presentation is some version of, Can I sell you something today? You benefit from coming across also as a vendor who asks, Can I learn a little more about you today? Because long-term vendor-customer relationships are so crucial in many business-to-business and technology markets, this is no small benefit.

Programmatic Visits for Market Research

In the 1980s (and maybe earlier) technology firms such as Hewlett-Packard began to experiment with a more systematic approach to customer visits in which 12, 20, or even 50 visits might be executed in order to address some topic of interest. The most common applications for such customer visit programs are new product development, new market development (i.e., selling an existing product line to a new type of customer or a new application), and customer satisfaction assessment. These programmatic visits are characterized by objectives set in advance, a carefully selected sample of customers, participation by cross-functional teams, a discussion guide used to direct the visit, an exploratory approach in asking questions, and a structured analysis and reporting process. What follows is an outline of the steps required to execute such a program:

Set objectives. A program of visits tends to devolve into a series of ad hoc visits unless objectives are set in advance. Examples of feasible objectives would include the following:

- Identify user needs.
- Explore customer perceptions concerning market events or trends.
- Generate ideas for product enhancement.
- Describe how customers make their purchase decision.

In general, any of the objectives that were deemed appropriate for exploratory research in Chapter 2 are appropriate for customer visits. The specific objectives should be hammered out in advance and regularly revisited during the program. It is surprising how often the team of people who participate in the visits do *not* initially agree on what the visits are supposed to accomplish. This occurs partly because customer visits are a highly flexible tool that can handle a wide variety of issues, and partly because it is often the only marketing research technique over which participants have any direct control. Hence, the visit program, unless checked, tends toward an "everything I wanted to know about customers but never had the chance to ask" orientation. For best results remember that less is more: fewer objectives, more thoroughly addressed, will generally be the best approach.

Select a sample. Sample selection is a make-or-break phase of program design. It doesn't matter how incisive your interviewing or insightful your analysis if you visit the wrong customers—people who don't deal with the issues that concern you, or are not part of the market you are trying to address. Garbage in–garbage out is the rule.

Begin by reviewing any segmentation scheme used by your business. This review of segments is important because you probably want to visit multiple instances of each important or relevant type of customer, *and* you want to avoid (for the visit program at hand) any kind of customer that is irrelevant to your objectives. For example, if your product is sold to four different industries, it may be important to visit customers from each; alternatively, if your product has half a dozen applications, and the changes you are contemplating only concern three of these applications, then you may want to include only customers with those applications in the sample. The end result of this first stage of sample selection is typically a list of three to six types of customers, yielding a tentative sample size of, in most cases, 12 to 36 visits (worldwide programs are generally somewhat larger, in the 30 to 60 range). In very concentrated markets, this list may name actual customer firms; in larger markets it is only a statement of types, such as national distributors with mainframe computers and a wide area network, batch manufacturers with local area networks, and so forth.

The point of going through this exercise is to avoid, first, the pitfalls of excluding customer types that are important to understand, second, wasting your time on customers who can't really help you, and third (the most subtle trap), always returning to visit the same small group of comfortable, familiar customers. One firm that neglected this latter point watched their market share slowly shrink even as their customer satisfaction ratings continued to go up and up (because they were doing an ever-better job of satisfying an ever-smaller niche of the market). Often the greatest discoveries and the most surprising insights come from visits made to less familiar customers, such as competitors' customers, or to customers who spend a lot on this product category but not very much on your product offering (which implies that from their perspective, something about your product is lacking).

The second phase of sample selection is specifying which job roles at the customer firm you want to visit. Most business-to-business products are bought and used by means of a group decision-making process that involves multiple individuals. If you only talk to one role—or worse, to different roles at different customers, thus confounding inter-role differences and inter-firm differences—you risk coming to a partial and misleading perspective on your market. An important part of the recruiting process is qualifying the persons you will be interviewing at the customer site. It is extremely disappointing to travel at great expense to a customer site and realize, in the first five minutes, that you are speaking to someone who has no involvement with your issues. Because customer visits are one of the very few market research techniques that allow you to understand multiple decision makers at a customer, and because group decision making is so characteristic of business-to-business markets, most customer visits should include multiple job roles at each customer. In many cases, this adds very little to the cost while substantially deepening the understanding gained. Recruiting itself can be handled by the program coordinator (common in concentrated markets with enduring vendor–customer relationships) or by an outside market research firm (common when customers are hard to find and also in close-to-mass-market situations with hundreds of thousands of buyers).

Select teams. The best teams are cross-functional—for example, a team that includes someone from marketing plus someone from engineering (in the case of new product development), or someone from quality control and someone from manufacturing engineering (in the case of customer satisfaction), and so forth. One reason for the superiority of teams is that a lot of work has to be done to make an interview effective, and one person can't do it all. A second reason is that cross-functional teams see with "stereo vision." Note that larger programs typically involve two or three teams to split up the work load, so that no one team has to visit more than 6 to 10 customers.

Devise a discussion guide. The guide is a two- to four-page document that functions as an agenda for the visit. In outline form it lists the major topics to be covered and under each topic reminds you of key questions to be asked and issues to watch for. The topics are arranged in a sequence that develops naturally and is comfortable for the customer. A discussion guide performs three valuable functions: it keeps you on track during each visit, it ensures consistency across visits, and it coordinates the efforts of multiple teams in large visits.

Conduct the interviews. You are *not* executing a survey in person; that is to say, you are not asking a fixed set of questions in a rigidly prescribed manner. Rather, you are engaged in a directed conversation with an expert informant—your customer. Exploration in depth is the focus. The two key skills to be mastered here are the creation of rapport and effective probing. You create rapport by demonstrating unconditional positive regard for the customer. Whether the customer delivers good news, bad news, or strange news, your attitude is constant: you are my customer and it is important that I understand you. You do not need to glad-hand the customer, and you should not try to maintain a poker face. You need only come across as committed to listening and learning.

To probe means to ask follow-up questions to extend and clarify initial answers. In this connection, open-ended questions that do not prestructure answers should be emphasized in customer visits (e.g., "What are you looking for in your next printer?," as opposed to a closed-ended question such as "Do you want two-sided printing in your next printer?"). Whenever you receive an answer to an open-ended question, your next question should almost invariably be some form of "Anything else/what else?" More generally, understand that customers, like other human beings, typically give vague, nonspecific, rambling, semicoherent answers to questions. To fully grasp the meaning of these answers requires effective probing.

Debrief the teams. Immediately after concluding the visit, it is important that the team be debriefed. In the beginning of the visit program, debriefing provides an opportunity to discuss changes to the discussion guide and interview procedure. Toward the conclusion, debriefing gives you a head start on the analysis, as you ask how today's visit compares and contrasts with previous visits. Throughout, debriefing provides a cross-check on each team member's perceptions of what customers are saying.

Analyze and report results. Analysis can be free form or structured. In free-form analysis a review of visit notes uncovers themes, contrasts, discoveries, and enumerations (i.e., customer needs or requirements identified through the visits). An example of a structured approach would be quality function deployment (QFD). Here matrices are generated to map customer requirements onto product features and engineering criteria.

It is fair to say that the quality of analysis of customer visit data depends heavily on the insight and industry experience of the person(s) analyzing the visit. Although no kind of market research ever eliminates the need for judgment and perspective, this need is particularly great in the case of customer visits.

Examples

Here are two examples of visit programs, one conducted by Sun Microsystems to better understand sources of customer satisfaction and dissatisfaction, and the other conducted by Apple Computer to explore the potential for a new product.

Sun Microsystems wanted to understand problems associated with a customer's first encounter with the company, specifically, from the point where the shipment of computers first arrived until the system was up and running. This effort was spearheaded by members of the company's quality function who perceived that the first encounter was sometimes more problematic than it had to be. Cross-functional teams conducted more than 50 visits worldwide, yielding a variety of insights that would be difficult or impossible to obtain in any other way. These ranged from the impact of the packaging used, to international differences in desk layout and office configuration, to subtle problems with the usability and installation of various pieces of equipment. Because solutions to many of these problems cut across departments and functions, the cross-functional makeup of the visit teams proved crucial in addressing identified problems.

The Display Products Division of Apple Computer Co. wanted to explore the potential for an entirely new product category that would expand the division's offerings. The goal of the visit program was to discover unmet needs that the present products did not satisfy, to describe customer requirements that the new product would have to meet, and to explore the fit between Apple's core competency and these requirements.

The division conducted more than 30 visits in the United States and Europe. A product manager from the marketing function coordinated the visits, and a wide range of scientists and engineers participated (the new product solution was much more than an incremental change or twist on an existing offering). Marketing managers combined information gained from these visits with secondary and other market research to help division management understand the issues surrounding the decision whether or not to invest in the new solution.

The visits yielded a wealth of data, summarized in profiles, about applications for the new product, problems with existing solutions, and perceptions of Apple's ability to deliver a successful solution. Design engineers came away from the visits with a clear vision of what the product had to do in order to succeed.

Cost

A good estimating procedure is to multiply the number of visits contemplated by $1,500 to account for direct travel costs incurred by a two-person team (airfare, hotel, car rental, meals). Programs with a substantial international component cost rather more; by contrast, programs in which all the visits are conducted locally by car have negligible out-of-pocket costs. Purely local programs are generally not a good idea, however, because your mental models are probably already overly shaped by local customers, and because there is often considerable geographical diversity in customer viewpoints, inasmuch as different industries are concentrated in different locales. One approach to controlling costs for out-of-town visits is to bunch several visits onto a single airfare, inasmuch as airfare is the major component of travel expense. Another is to piggyback research visits onto existing trips: if you are already scheduled to go to Atlanta for a conference, why not stay an extra day or two and conduct several visits as part of a program that will span a month or two?

Strengths and Weaknesses

The customer visit technique has several key strengths that combine to position visits just behind secondary research as a general all-purpose market research tool. First, visits are field research. They take you out of your world and put you into the customer's world. Second, visits take the form of face-to-face interaction. Research has shown that face-to-face is the richest of all communication modes, in the sense of being best able to handle complex, ambiguous, and novel information. Third, the combination of field study and face-to-face communication is ideal for entering into the customer's thought world—the customer's perspective and priorities. Being able to think like a customer is perhaps the core marketing competency, and customer visits provide one of the best means of helping nonmarketing functions such as engineering to envision their customers. Fourth, customer visits provide information that is gained first-hand, directly. As someone remarked to me, "Everyone believes his or her own eyes and ears over others." Customer visits can sometimes be helpful in changing hearts and minds because the evidence of an unsatisfied need is so much more vivid and compelling when gathered this way. Overall, the distinctive strength of customer visits is depth of understanding. For instance, you can spend a whole hour nailing down exactly what goes on in a particular application or process. Sustained dialogue gives you the picture seen from multiple reinforcing angles, in a way that a table of cross-tabulated survey responses never will.

The great weakness of customer visits is the potential for interviewer bias. If you have spent six months slaving over a design concept, will you really be able to listen to and explore the response of that customer whose initial reaction is something along the lines of "what a silly idea"? Historically the consensus of academic opinion was that managers could not be trusted to conduct their own market research; rather, the combination of greater objectivity and expertise made outside professionals the superior choice. Perhaps a more balanced perspective would be that although bias is a constant danger, nonetheless the advantages listed in the preceding paragraph compel the involvement of managers and other decision makers in customer visits. Given this realization, one can act to control bias in two ways: first, by the use of teams (although my bias is invisible to me, it is painfully apparent to you!), and second, by following up customer visits with other more controlled procedures, such as survey research, choice modeling, and experimentation.

The second abiding weakness of customer visits is the instability and imprecision consequent to small sample sizes. Often there is a great temptation to treat a customer visit program as a kind of survey, and to report such findings as "75% of our customers had a positive reaction to adding this piece of functionality," or "only one customer in eight reporting having problems with X." Just a little statistical reflection reveals that in a random sample of 16 customers, the 95% confidence interval around an estimate of "75% agreement" extends from about 53% to 97%, and that in the nonrandom samples typically used for customer visits, this confidence interval must be wider still. If you want the kind of precision that percentages imply, you need a large sample survey. Where customer visits excel is in explaining *why* some customers had a favorable reaction to a piece of functionality, and not in estimating the proportion of customers who have that reaction.

Do's and Don'ts

Do get engineers and other nonmarketers involved in customer visits.

Don't confine yourself to a conference room. Walk around and observe. Soak up the total picture of this customer's operation.

Do enlist the support and cooperation of the local field sales organization. They can do so much to frustrate or assist your purpose. They know these customers well and can add perspective to what you hear.

Don't ask customers for solutions—ask them to identify problems that need solving. The customer is the authority on what the real problems are, but the vendor is the authority on what a profitable solution to those problems might be.

Don't talk too much. You are there to listen. The more you talk, the more you shape customer responses and the less your chances of making a discovery or being surprised.

Do use visual aids. Diagrams, short lists, and the like help the customer to focus on the total idea to which you want reactions.

Do use verbatim quotes from customers in reports. Customers often express themselves more vividly and with less inhibition than you would allow yourself.

Suggested Readings

Burchill, Gary, and Christina Hepner-Brodie. 1997. *Voices into Choices: Acting on the Voice of the Customer.* Boston: Joiner-Oriel.

Like Miles and Huberman (see below), the focus here is on what happens after the visits, but this book is much more focused on process, including organizational challenges and issues that have to be confronted.

Griffin, Abbie, and John R. Hauser. 1993. The voice of the customer. *Marketing Science* 12(1): 1–27.

Addresses a number of issues associated with conducting customer visits, in particular the necessary sample size.

Guillart, Francis J., and Frederick D. Sturdivant. 1994. Spend a day in the life of your customer. *Harvard Business Review* (January/February): 116–125.

Describes some uses of inbound customer visits and clarifies the kind of perspective customers are uniquely qualified to give.

Iansiti, Marco, and Stein, Ellen. 1995. *Understanding User Needs,* HBS #9-695-091. Cambridge, MA: HBS Publishing.

Explains the role played by customer visits, focus groups, and other techniques in product development.

McQuarrie, Edward F. 1998. *Customer Visits: Building a Better Market Focus,* 2nd ed. Newbury Park, CA: Sage.

McQuarrie, Edward F. 1995. Taking a road trip: Customer visits help companies recharge relationships and pass competitors. *Marketing Management* 3: 8–21.

My book offers a complete step-by-step guide to designing, conducting, and analyzing a program of visits. The article offers a condensed version of this chapter, with an emphasis on ad hoc visits.

Miles, M. B., and A. M. Huberman. 1994. *Qualitative Data Analysis: An Expanded Sourcebook.* Thousand Oaks, CA: Sage.

This book addresses the issue of what to do with qualitative customer visit data once you have it. This area of inquiry has become much more active in recent years, and a search of Amazon.com for books on qualitative data analysis supplies plenty of additional leads.

Shapiro, Benson. 1988. What the hell is "market-oriented"? *Harvard Business Review* 66 (November-December): 119–125.

Shows how customer visits can be used to turn around a stagnant organization and make it more market-focused.

von Hippel, Eric. 1990. *The Sources of Innovation.* New York: Oxford University Press.

Describes what can be learned from visits to lead users—creative, knowledgeable customers who are adapting existing products to novel uses.

5

The Focus Group

The term *focus group* is sometimes used loosely to cover any group interview. Strictly speaking, however, in the world of market research a focus group is a particular kind of group interview supported by a specialized infrastructure. This infrastructure includes (1) the facility, (2) the market research vendor, and (3) the moderator.

The facility is typically an independent small business that has at least one specialized meeting room. This room has a table large enough to seat a dozen consumers, a one-way mirror from behind which observers can view the proceedings, and the capacity to audio- and videotape the group. The facility typically is located in a shopping mall or office building.

The market research vendor is generally a separate business entity responsible for coordinating the entire focus group research project. The three specific responsibilities of the vendor are to find a facility, supply a moderator who will lead the groups, and arrange for consumers to be recruited to attend (both the moderator and the recruiter may themselves be separate business entities; often the facility handles recruiting in addition to hosting the group). The value added by the vendor is fundamentally that provided by any middleman or broker: the vendor consults with you to design an appropriate research strategy, brings together all the external resources required to implement the study, and then drives the process to its conclusion.

The moderator is an individual with general skills in conducting interviews and specific skills in managing group interaction. Virtually all focus group moderators also conduct one-on-one interviews, but not all people who conduct one-on-one interviews are capable of running a focus group. Interviewing a group is more demanding. In addition to leading the group, the moderator also works with the client before the group to refine the objectives for the discussion, and is typically, but not always, the analyst who writes the report on the groups (some vendors separate the moderating and analysis tasks).

If the infrastructure as just described is not present, it is probably best to refer to your research study as simply a group interview in order to avoid confusion.

Procedure

1. You send out a request for proposals (RFP) to several market research vendors outlining the kind of customers you want recruited, the number of groups you expect to be held (three or four is typical), and the issues and topics to be explored in the group.

2. The selected vendor recommends a facility (often groups are held in two or more cities to encompass regional differences in consumer response), puts you in touch with a moderator, and prepares for your review the screener that will be used by phone recruiters.

3. You edit the screener, which consists of four to five questions designed to make sure that the consumers who are recruited are in fact the right kind of people for your purposes. For example, if you are a computer manufacturer exploring the needs of computer users who work at home, the screener will be designed to ensure that each participant (a) does work at home for some minimum number of hours; (b) does have a computer; and (c) does use that computer as part of working at home. The screener might also ensure that one or more applications is present, for example, that a spreadsheet is used. Finally, the screener might be used to build a mix into the group: to recruit three or four users of Linux, three or four users of Windows, and two or three Apple Macintosh users as part of an 8- to 10-person focus group.

4. Phone recruiting commences. Many calls have to be made to get a person on the line. Some of these people prove to be ineligible, and some of the remaining are not interested. As recruiting proceeds, you review the completed screeners to make sure the right kinds of people are being recruited.

5. Meanwhile, you meet with the moderator to develop the discussion guide. Typically you have written a memo describing the topics and issues to be raised in the group discussion and some specific questions to be asked. The moderator transforms this into a discussion guide that

functions as an agenda for the group. The discussion guide indicates how topics are sequenced and how questions are worded.

6. You and any of your colleagues who will be attending the focus group meet with the moderator at the facility an hour before the group is scheduled to begin. As consumers arrive, you stay in touch with the facility host/hostess to double-check eligibility and to make snap decisions about whom to include if a surplus of people actually show up. Consumers are generally served food while they wait.

7. The group session lasts 1½ to 2 hours. You have the opportunity to send in one or two notes and to briefly huddle with the moderator before the wrap-up. After each group (two are generally held in an evening), alterations can be made to the discussion guide.

8. After the last group the moderator or analyst spends one to three weeks preparing a report which varies in length according to what you're willing to pay. Longer reports contain verbatim quotes drawn from the tapes. You may also choose to have a summary videotape made that contains 10 to 15 minutes of particularly insightful discussion.

Cost Factors

For business-to-business groups, budget for $5,000 to $12,000 per group and a three-group minimum. It is somewhat rare to see a project that includes more than six groups, so you can assume that most focus group projects will cost between $15,000 and $72,000. Costs go up with the difficulty of locating respondents, and with the dollar amount required to incentivize them to participate. Hence, groups conducted with a specialized population of affluent individuals can cost four to five times as much as groups conducted with ordinary consumers.

Examples

The first example is a business that made small handheld testing equipment used by customers whose factories manufactured a variety of electrical systems. The product in question was one among many made by the division, which in turn was part of a large, well-known multinational firm. Although the product had been offered for decades in one form or another, it had never been the leading brand in its market.

A strategic review indicated it was time to develop a new generation of the product to reflect advances in technology. Product marketing staff argued for focus groups as an initial stage of market research. Staff members pointed out that objective measures of product performance and business strength did not square with the product's weak market position. Something else must be going on, and if the next generation of the product was to succeed, this "something else" had to be understood.

Four focus groups were conducted with technicians and engineers who used this product in the course of their work. The screeners used in recruitment ensured that users of several brands, including the company's own, were present. Given the firm's weak position in the market, however, a majority of those who attended were users of other brands. The use of an outside research vendor ensured that the sponsoring firm remained anonymous. This contributed to a frank and candid atmosphere in the groups.

The group discussions, which were viewed by marketing staff and engineering management, were like a bucket of cold water. Some quite harsh and belittling comments were made about the sponsor and its product. Comments such as "Overengineered and overpriced" and "Way too delicate for use on the factory floor" give some indication of the tone. Intriguingly, the charge of fragility had no basis in objective fact. Engineering analyses had shown the product to be no less sturdy or durable than its competitors. Rather, fragility was an inference made by potential customers based on how the product's casing looked and felt.

The focus groups had a salutary effect on management—a "wake-up call" as one marketer put it. A 15-minute video containing highlights was widely shown and had a galvanizing effect. Both customer visits and a descriptive survey were subsequently undertaken to extend and confirm the results of the focus group. The new product designed in light of this research was extremely successful in the marketplace, with the result that the leading brand lost a substantial chunk of its market share.

The second example comes from a large computer manufacturer that undertook research to better understand the issue of software quality. Although the firm had always had a commitment to making high-quality products, the growing importance of software to its revenue stream, in combination with an emerging emphasis on total quality, suggested a need for exploratory market research. In particular, corporate quality control staff had the uneasy sense that quality had come to be too narrowly defined as errors per line of code, and was seeking to understand the customer's perspective on the meaning of quality.

Eight focus groups were conducted as part of what was intended to be a two-stage research project, where the second stage would be a large-scale choice modeling study designed to identify the importance of each of the quality attributes identified in the focus groups, and to assess the perceived quality delivered by each major competitor. Although some members of the corporate market research staff had wanted to move immediately to the choice modeling study, quality control staff insisted on doing focus groups first, out of a sense that too many issues remained undefined.

Two groups each were conducted in Boston, New York, Atlanta, and San Francisco. Four groups concerned engineering or technical software applications (e.g., computer-aided design), and four groups concerned general commercial applications (e.g., word processing, accounting). For both the commercial and engineering software sets, two groups consisted of ordinary software users, one group consisted of management information system (MIS) directors responsible for supporting such users, and one group consisted of independent software consultants and software suppliers. Screening during recruitment ensured that users of large and small computers, users of the firm's own software and other brands, and employees of large and small businesses would be included.

The groups proved valuable in several respects. First, the customer perspective on quality became much more richly articulated. Diverse attributes of quality, such as "robust" and "intuitive," which had been little more than catch phrases before, were elaborated with examples, clarifications, and contrasts. Second, the term *software quality* proved to hold virtually no meaning for the typical user. Blank stares were a typical reaction when the moderator introduced this term in the early groups. Components of the software product, such as manuals or help screens, sometimes elicited energetic discussion of good or bad, but *software quality* per se was not a concept that users could easily define. Third, likes and dislikes proved very heterogeneous across users— whatever software quality was, it was not one unvarying thing. Fourth and most important, most users were familiar with only one brand of software—the one they used. Competitive products had essentially no visibility in most cases.

As a result of the groups, the anticipated large-scale choice modeling study was canceled. The particular study under consideration required ratings of competitor products—a task that would clearly be impossible for users in light of the focus group discussions. Hence, the focus group project yielded two benefits. The corporate quality staff's understanding of software quality from the customer's perspective was greatly enriched, and an expensive and ill-advised quantitative market research study, costing many tens of thousands of dollars more than the focus group study, was avoided.

Strengths and Weaknesses

The great strength of the focus group technique is its capacity to produce surprise and a fresh perspective. Because the interview is minimally structured, because participants react to and provoke one another, and because the moderator drives the group to reflect and explore, there is a high probability that management will hear something new and unexpected. Hence, focus groups make a great deal of sense *early* in a market research project.

The unique strength of the focus group is that it brings multiple customers into direct interaction with one another. It is customary to extol the "synergy" that results. However, this rather vague term can be given a much more precise definition drawing on theories from social psychology. Two fundamental processes occur in discussion groups composed of strangers: groups *unify* and groups *polarize*. That is, initially strangers brought together in a group seek common ground; subsequently, they polarize into factions.

This twin dynamic has powerful implications for market research using focus groups. Because of the unification dynamic, focus groups are very useful when exploring a new market or getting back in touch with an old market. Thus, if your computer company is expanding into a hospital market, and you convene a focus group of 10 nurses, these nurses will re-create "nurse world" within the group. The unification dynamic makes the *common denominator* visible. Because of the polarization dynamic, focus groups are also useful in identifying possible segment boundaries. In the process of dividing into factions, customers in the group reveal what makes them *different* from one another. This is helpful because it prevents premature closure—you discover that one size does not fit all. Focus groups may be the only market research technique where customers have the opportunity to challenge, argue with, and dissent from one another in ways that an interviewer would never dare undertake in a one-on-one interview. This can reveal the extent to which people are committed to diverse views.

Finally, focus groups have a number of minor advantages that can be useful in certain circumstances. In the United States, at least, the identity of the sponsor need not be revealed to participants (this is not always the case overseas). This can be most useful when you want to hear frank and candid assessments of your brand as compared with others. Customer visits—the major alternative to focus groups when exploratory research is desired—do not enjoy this advantage. Another useful feature is that focus groups occur in a concentrated time interval. Busy high-level managers are much more likely to show up for two evenings, and thus view four focus groups, than they are to accompany you on the week of travel required to make six customer visits. Because the focus group can be unobtrusively videotaped, you can, by creating and circulating an edited "highlights" tape, expose a large number of employees to almost direct customer input.

The most important weakness of the focus group technique is one that it shares with customer visits and other exploratory tools: the reliance on small, nonrandom samples. Because the sample is small and may or may not reflect the larger population of consumers in the market, the kinds of conclusions you can draw from focus group research are limited. You can *never* confidently extrapolate a percentage or frequency from a group. Thus, it is never appropriate to conclude from groups that "consumers preferred concept A to concept B by a two-to-one margin." Note that this difficulty does not in any way diminish if one adopts a loose and imprecise manner of speaking. "Only a few consumers see problems with . . ." is just as illegitimate an extrapolation as "Only 12% of consumers see problems with . . ." The judgment "only a few" draws exactly the same quantitative inference from the focus group sample as "only 12%." Neither is justified when the representativeness of the sample is unknown.

It might be objected, "Well, what good are focus groups, then?" Although focus groups can never estimate the *frequency* of some consumer judgment, preference, or response, they can reveal the fact of its existence and illuminate its nature. To refer back to the first example application given above, the focus group revealed the fact that one or more real customers believed that the product was overengineered and overpriced, and the fact that some viewed it to be fragile. Ensuing discussion also revealed possible sources for such beliefs and their position within the network of other beliefs. However, were these beliefs held by a *few* idiosyncratic customers, by *some group* of customers, or by *many* customers? There was no way to know until follow-up research was conducted. All management could know based on groups alone was the nature and character of those beliefs, together with the fact that at least *some* customers held them. If those beliefs and their exact nature came as a surprise, then the groups paid for themselves. If managers had already known (and taken seriously) all these things, then the groups would have proved a waste of time.

Focus groups suffer from a number of other weaknesses that are distinctive and not shared with other kinds of exploratory research. Most of these stem from the very fact that a group is involved. Specifically, focus groups are quite vulnerable to logistical foul-ups. Traffic jams, random events, customers' busy schedules, and so forth, may produce a higher-than-expected number of no-shows. It is hard to do a focus group when only three people actually show up. Worse, most of the money spent is irretrievably lost.

More generally, focus groups are vulnerable to dominant individuals who monopolize the conversation, to shy individuals who withdraw, and to bandwagon effects, where group members simply acquiesce with an initial vehemently stated position. A good moderator can control many of these effects, but they remain liabilities.

The group synergy characteristic of focus groups also has a downside: limits on airtime. In a two-hour group with eight people, an average of 15 minutes of airtime is available to each person. Can you learn everything you need to know from an individual customer in 15 minutes? For many relatively simple consumer products, the answer may well be yes; but for business-to-business and technology products the answer may be no, in which case, customer visits should be examined as an alternative. Also because of airtime restrictions, focus groups are an inferior idea-generation technique. Research has shown that interviews with 32 individuals yield more and better ideas than four focus groups with eight people each. Of course, focus groups may be a *satisfactory* idea-generation technique, even though not a superior one (especially given the time savings associated with conducting four groups versus 32 individual interviews). But focus groups are probably better suited to examining a few key topics in depth than to generating a wide variety of ideas.

Lastly, the use of a professional moderator is both a strength and a weakness. The moderator contributes interviewing skills plus detachment and objectivity. The downside, for many technology and business-to-business marketers, concerns the moderator's ability to quickly assimilate the essentials of your business situation and the technical specifics of your product. Absent that understanding, the moderator is not going to be able to effectively probe topics raised in the groups.

The fact that the profession of moderator continues to exist suggests that individuals who take this career path tend to be quick studies who can assimilate the necessary knowledge, client after client. On the other hand, the complexity of some technology products is such that I have encountered businesses that have soured on focus groups precisely because of their experiences with moderators who could not effectively probe key issues. If your product fits this profile, it is crucial that you be comfortable that the moderator you intend to use has the requisite understanding. Otherwise, customer visits are a fallback technique.

Do's and Don'ts

Do invite key players in different functional areas to view the groups. Much important thinking and discussion occurs behind the one-way mirror.

Do monitor the telephone screening of potential participants. Look at the completed screeners and ask yourself if this is in fact the kind of person you are hoping will attend.

Do vet the moderator—so much depends on this person's skill.

Don't count responses. Don't take votes seriously (votes are okay as a springboard for further discussion: it is when you draw inferences about the population of customers based on the vote that the trouble begins).

Don't distribute and analyze questionnaires. It is okay to get additional background information to help interpret the responses of participants, but it is not okay to treat the people who happen to attend the groups as grist for an almost-free survey.

Don't stop with one group or two. If focus groups are worth doing at all, you should do three or more.

Don't make the recruiting parameters too ambitious. This drives up the cost and may cause recruiting to fail altogether. It also suggests that you are seeking a precision that focus groups can't give.

Suggested Readings

Fern, Edward F. 2002. *Advanced Focus Group Research.* Thousand Oaks, CA: Sage.

This book has no parallel in the extensive literature on focus groups. It is the first attempt to provide a comprehensive conceptual and theoretical account of what can be learned from the focus group considered as a social science methodology. Although addressed primarily to the academic reader, it is accessible to thoughtful practitioners as well.

Goldman, Alfred E., and Susan Schwartz McDonald. 1987. *The Group Depth Interview: Principles and Practice.* New York: Prentice Hall.

Langer, Suzanne. 2001. *The Mirrored Window: Focus Groups from a Moderator's Point of View.* New York: PMP.

These two books are an excellent resource for moderators who want to improve their skills. If you are a person who will have occasion to conduct group interviews from time to time, you also will find useful advice. Goldman and McDonald are particularly strong on the psychological aspects of group interviews.

Greenbaum, Thomas. 1997. *The Handbook for Focus Group Research,* 2nd ed. Thousand Oaks, CA: Sage.

Probably the best book for the businessperson who uses focus groups for purposes of making a business decision. Greenbaum covers the whole phenomenon, and has some particularly interesting chapters on future trends and careers as a focus group moderator.

Morgan, David L. 1996. *Focus Groups as Qualitative Research,* 2nd ed. Newbury Park, CA: Sage.

The author, a sociologist, addresses a different audience than the other books named: scholars who will use focus groups as part of their scholarship. This orientation also makes the book useful as an assignment to students who will conduct focus groups as part of a research project. Because Morgan disdains the need for the infrastructure described at the beginning of the chapter, the book is also useful to those who, for cost or other reasons, will not have access to that infrastructure.

6

Sampling

Sampling is one of those key technical skills that does not form part of a general manager's skill set, but that is central to competence in market research. Because it rests on specific, narrow technical skills, it will be outsourced in most real-world cases. The market research vendor, or perhaps even an independent consultant retained by that vendor, will devise the sample plan. Given this book's goal of offering only a concise introduction to market research, this chapter, more than most, only skims the surface of the actual procedures required to select and size a sample in any real-world case. By contrast, the typical market research textbook devotes several chapters to the topic of sampling, and begins the treatment with a review of the fundamentals of probability, essentially recapitulating a portion of the statistics courses required of all business students. Although it is almost certainly true that one cannot really understand sampling without a solid grounding in the basics of probability distributions, that traditional approach is not appropriate in the context of this book.

The goals of this chapter are limited. The first goal is to prevent or at least minimize bewilderment in connection with the topic of sampling. General managers are going to sit in meetings where terms like *probability sample* get tossed around, in a context where the basic question reduces to How much money do we need to spend? (a question that is very much the province of general managers). Interestingly, engineering managers often need help avoiding bewilderment in these same conversations. Although engineers get exposed to plenty of high-level math in most engineering curricula, the math that underlies sampling approaches in the context of social science tends to be quite different from the math that underlies physics, and, at least initially, unfamiliar to the trained engineer.

The second goal of this chapter is to enable a modicum of critical thinking about samples in the context of both proposed research and completed research. With proposed research, critical thinking about the kind of sample required facilitates a more effective research design. Critical thinking about the samples used in completed studies, such as those found in secondary research, helps you decide which findings deserve the most weight, or should have any credibility at all. There really are a lot of bad samples out there in the world! Awareness of this fact, combined with an understanding of what makes a sample good or bad, fosters a healthy skepticism that serves a general manager well.

In light of these limited goals, this chapter has two sections: a discussion of the basic kinds of samples and their key advantages and disadvantages, followed by a discussion of how to estimate the needed sample size when conditions are straightforward. Determination of sample size is where the rubber hits the road in commercial market research; it is a key cost driver and may determine the feasibility of a given research project.

A final limitation on this chapter's discussion is that we will generally assume that you are seeking to sample human beings. Fascinating problems and challenges of great interest to the professional statistician arise when the goal is to sample something other than humans from within a larger group of humans. For instance, one might need instead to sample from the population of sales calls in the third fiscal quarter, from retail transactions occurring at stores in a given region, from highway intersections in the state of California, from truck trips between your warehouse and distributors, and so forth. However, the complexities that would be introduced if the treatment had to be sufficiently general to cover all sorts of sampling tasks would undercut our limited goals. Hence, I assume throughout that you intend to sample individual customers.

Types of Samples

A few definitions may help. A *population* is the total set of people that results obtained from the sample are supposed to reflect. Populations can be of any size or level of generality, for instance, all residents of the United States, all U.S. households with phone service, all persons who own a hydro-widget, all purchasers of *our* brand of hydro-widget, all our hydro-widget accounts who purchased more than 10 hydro-widgets in the past 24 months, and so forth. Sometimes multiple populations may be involved in the research, such as domestic versus international hydro-widget owners, or widget accounts in sales territory one versus those in sales territory two.

The *initial* sample is that limited number of people within the population who are contacted to participate in the research. If the population is so small and our effort so diligent that we can contact all of them (e.g., all our widget accounts that were opened in the first fiscal quarter), then there is no sample—we refer to this as a census of the population. Continuing in this vein, the *obtained* sample is the people within the initial sample that actually completed the research. Finally, the sample frame is the device we use to access the population to draw a sample. A mailing list is a simple example of a sample frame (e.g., members of the National Association of Widget Operatives). The subset of all 10-digit numbers, where the first three numbers correspond to telephone area codes now in use, would be a more subtle example of a sample frame.

Probability Sample or Nonprobability Sample?

This is the single most important thing to understand: some samples are probability samples, and these have special advantages; all other samples are nonprobability samples and lack these advantages. Don't misunderstand—the category of "good" samples, in the sense of suitable to the task at hand, includes nonprobability samples as well as probability samples; but nonprobability samples are good samples only in circumstances where the advantages enjoyed by probability samples are not required, or are outweighed by their disadvantages (as when probability samples have the property of being impossible to obtain—a very big disadvantage).

You are likely to be more familiar with the term *random sample* than with the term *probability sample*, but simple random samples are only one kind of probability sample. The property that distinguishes probability samples, and that gives them their peculiar advantage, is that every member of the population has a known or calculable probability of ending up in the initial sample. Thus, if we use a random number table to construct seven-digit phone numbers within an area code we know that there is one chance in 9,999,999 that any given phone number would appear in the sample (assuming that all the possible three-number prefixes are in use). Similarly, if we obtain from the Internal Revenue Service a list of all foundations that filed a tax return in 2003, and contact every 50th name on the list, we would also have a probability sample (of foundations that filed). Note that the second example is not a random sample—you have to use a random number table or its equivalent to claim to have a random sample. The second instance is referred to as a *systematic sample*, and because of the prevalence of lists in market research, and the unwieldy nature of random number tables, systematic samples are probably more common than strictly random samples.

The advantage enjoyed by probability samples is that if one additional piece of information is known (the "variance," to be defined later) we can calculate a margin of error, for a given sample size, for any numerical value that we obtain from the sample. The importance of this property can be grasped if we permutate the preceding sentence slightly: if we know our allowable margin of error, then we can calculate the exact size needed for our sample. With a probability sample, we can say to a general manager, "If you can tell me how precise the research results need to be, I can tell you exactly what the sample size has to be." Knowing the precise sample size required means you can decide whether the research is feasible from a cost standpoint, and you can proceed in confidence that you have spent not one dollar more than is necessary.

Put another way, if you will be happy with a percentage breakdown that is within 10 percentage points of the true value, you will generally have to pay for only a small sample; if you require that results be within five percentage points, or two points, then you will generally have to pay for much larger samples. Of course, many people recognize intuitively that more precision requires a larger sample, all else being equal. The advantage of probability samples is that we can quantify that intuition. This means we can quantify "small, but adequate for our purposes" as precisely 300 respondents (not 100 and not 250), in some given case. And, most important, we can quantify "if we increase the size of the sample by this much, it will be more precise to about this degree." It makes a huge practical difference if "larger" means 500 instead of 300 respondents— or if it means 7,000 instead of 300 respondents, as in the example at the beginning of this paragraph, where we tightened the margin of error from 10 points to 2.

In short, probability samples allow us to derive the needed sample size, with the huge practical advantages that confers. In addition, technically speaking virtually all statistical analyses commonly applied to market research data assume that the sample being analyzed is a probability sample of the population of interest. Only with probability samples can we be certain, to a known degree, that the sample *represents* (is similar to, allows us to project results to) the population. And it is that population that constitutes the market that we seek to understand.

Why Nonprobability Samples?

If nonprobability samples can't be sized mathematically, don't have a known margin of error, and don't technically permit the generalization of statistical analyses to the population, why would one ever bother with them? The answer, in the context of survey research and most other quantitative market research, is that there is no good reason to settle for less than a probability sample! The only exception is if a good probability sample cannot be obtained (in which case, the whole project of undertaking quantitative market research needs to be reviewed).

Interestingly enough, qualitative research does *not* require probability samples. Understanding why this is so is useful, both for understanding sampling and for understanding what qualitative market research can and cannot do. First, the main types of nonprobability samples that occur in market research may be termed convenience samples, quota samples, and judgment samples. Convenience samples are by and large worthless. A good example of a convenience sample would be your boss's boss saying, "I had golf with Joe yesterday. He's a big buyer of our widgets and he suggested configuring the product this way." In this example, Joe is a convenience sample. If your boss's boss is an avid golfer and adds Harry, Sue, and Tom to the list of large customers desiring a certain configuration, this expanded convenience sample is about as bad as the sample that consisted of Joe alone. In my opinion, if you are contemplating using only a convenience sample for a quantitative market research study, you might as well skip the market research and just do what you want.

To envision a quota sample, imagine interviewers with clipboards in a shopping mall. They are told to complete 100 interviews with shoppers, and to be sure that 50 are with women, 50 with men, and that half the interviewees from each gender should be older than 30 and half younger. In this way, quotas are set for the obtained sample. The disability of quota samples, relative to probability samples, is easily seen in this case. If patrons of the mall are not split evenly between male and female, young and old, then we are forcing a distribution onto the sample. Oversampling the comparatively rare male shopper under 30 is not going to give us a representative sample of males under 30 in the population. Almost by definition, these rarely found young male shoppers are unrepresentative of their population segment! Even if the quotas match the population (we want the sample to be one half hydro-widget operators, one third xeri-widget operators, and one sixth turbo-widget operators, because secondary research shows that's how the market is segmented), there are still too many noise variables that intrude when we take a close look at how quota samples are actually obtained. Thus, which under-30 male do you suppose gets approached for an interview in that shopping mall study: the short skinny one with glasses, wearing a white shirt and tie; or the large mustachioed one wearing a tank top and carrying a boom box? All such factors make it less likely that we can project results from the quota sample to the population of interest.

In a judgment sample you use your best judgment to draw the sample. In the context of focus group recruiting, you might reason as follows: "For these groups on wireless networks for the home, let's screen for either a DSL or cable subscription. Plus, to be eligible they need to have at least two computers at home. Let's also make sure that at least one third of each group owns a Macintosh. Let's do half the groups in newly built Sunbelt suburbs and half in older northeastern cities where masonry construction is common, so we can get a handle on wiring and installation issues." It's called a *judgment sample* because in your best judgment, restricting the sample as described (e.g., must have a broadband connection), and ensuring a dispersion across other variables (e.g., Mac or PC ownership) will yield a group of people all of whom will be able to speak to the issues of concern. Now, to what extent will a tabulation of responses heard in these groups be representative of the population of purchasers and potential purchasers of home wireless networking systems? It is impossible to calculate, and that's the point. Rather, in your judgment, people qualified in this way will yield more useful information than would a random sample of adult citizens, a systematic sample from your set of warranty cards, or a random sample of broadband customers, and more information relative to any other judgment sample that you could conceive (i.e., one that specified that all participants should have a graduate degree, annual household incomes over $150,000, and no one in the household with an engineering or technical degree). If your judgment is good, then the sample obtained will not be bad, or not as bad as other alternatives. But the goodness of your judgment and hence the projectability of results obtained with this sample cannot be calculated. Judgment samples are not probability samples.

Qualitative Research and Judgment Samples

With these distinctions among types of samples in hand, we can return to the issue of the different kinds of samples required for quantitative as opposed to qualitative research. The factor that drives *quantitative* researchers to seek out probability samples is the desire to generalize from sample values to population values with a predetermined precision. And it is true that for a certain kind of generalization, it is imperative that probability samples be used. Specifically, if we want to generalize from the relative or absolute incidence of some response in the sample, to the incidence of that same response in the population, then a probability sample is required. Typically, this is exactly what we want to do with the results of a survey or an experiment. If 27% of a sample of broadband users anticipate purchasing a wireless networking base station in the next year, we want to be able to conclude that 27% of that population, or 1.45 million households, are planning such a purchase. This allows us to calculate market size in dollars, given an average base station price (e.g., at $100, the base station market would be projected to be $145 million). Similarly, if 20% of the group that received direct mail headline A responded to the promotional offer, and only 12% of the group who received headline B did, we want to infer that we will have

		INCIDENCE										
		0%	10%	20%	30%	40%	50%	60%	70%	80%	90%	100%
I D E N T I F I C A T I O N	Quality 1											
	Quality 2											
	Quality 3											
	.											
	.											
	.											
	Quality K											

Figure 6.1   Two Axes of Generalization from Sample Data

more success if headline A is used on all 632,000 households on our master list than if headline B is used. The kind of generalization desired in these two examples might be termed an *incidence generalization.* This incidence generalization is shown as the horizontal axis in Figure 6.1.

As a general rule, one cannot reliably make incidence generalizations from qualitative research, or in the absence of probability samples generally. To explain why a probability sample is a requirement for incidence generalization we would have to go into the mathematics of probability distributions, which I promised this chapter would not do. So here you must take my word for it, or consult the suggested readings.

The important point for our purposes is that there is another kind of generalization that one might wish to make from sample data. This might be termed an *identification* generalization, corresponding to the vertical axis in Figure 6.1. What we want to do here is to conclude that some set of K elements identified to be present in the sample is also present in the population. In other words, we wish to generalize from the fact that exactly K elements appeared in the sample to the fact that the same K elements will be reasonably frequent in the population (and that no elements reasonably frequent in the population will be absent from the sample). The assumptions are that K is a relatively small number, on the order of 10 or fewer, and that "reasonably frequent in the population" means having a true incidence of 10% or more.

To translate this into practical terms, we may be more interested in identifying purchase motivations with respect to wireless networking equipment than in quantifying the incidence of purchase intentions. That is, rather than estimating the size of the base station market, we may want to identify reasons why people might want to purchase a wireless network in the first place. The assumption is that there are half a dozen distinct reasons, and maybe more, each of which is a driver for some fraction of total purchases. The further assumption is that we don't know the identity yet of all six reasons. We think we know one or two, and we suspect others, but our purpose in embarking on qualitative research is to get a firm grip on the range and character of purchase motivations in the wireless networking space.

Identification generalizations are characteristic of qualitative research; in fact, this term provides some formal meaning for the objective of discovery, the underlying motivation for much qualitative research. That is, we undertake customer visits and especially focus groups to identify the various *qualities* of consumer response (the K items) that are prevalent—that's why it is called *qualitative* research. We undertake quantitative research, especially survey research, to estimate *quantities*—the incidence in the population of known qualities of consumer response. In the estimation of quantities, or incidence, precision is everything, and probability samples are decisively superior. In the discovery of qualities, exhaustive identification, within the limits stated, is the goal, and judgment and quota samples are often adequate to this purpose.

For an intuitive demonstration of the adequacy of judgment samples for purposes of identity generalizations, let's invoke the classic example of beads drawn from an urn. First, let's review the traditional account, which concerns incidence generalizations. When incidence generalization is the goal, we seek to conclude, with known precision, what proportion of white or black beads is present in this urn. We need to know whether black beads are 35%, 45%, or 55% of the total, and we want to know the margin of error for our estimation. The mathematics of probability distributions indicates that a random draw of beads, of reasonable size (>30), will reliably indicate, with a margin of error of ±5 percentage points, the incidence of white and black beads in the urn. By the way, the math doesn't change much if we assume multiple colors of beads.

When identity generalization is the goal, the task is to identify how many colors of beads are present, with reasonable frequency, in the urn. With judgment samples, metaphorically speaking we get to walk around the urn (blindfolded, of course), and plunge our hands in at various points in the urn, and even rake them across the surface of the contents, plus we can reach to various depths, using our judgment to ensure that our hands pluck beads from multiple regions of the urn. To continue the metaphor, if we're doing four focus groups, we get to grab four double handfuls of beads. If it's 24 customer visits, then it's 24 small handfuls. We are drawing handfuls, not individual beads, to reflect the fact that any one customer can generally speak to multiple qualities of response, that is, several different reasons for purchasing a wireless home network. We represent focus groups as double handfuls to reflect the stimulative effect of group interaction.

Given that our purpose is identity generalization, how probable is it, given that green beads are 10% of the urn's contents, that the handfuls we draw will contain at least one green bead? Well, since we didn't draw a probability sample of beads, there is no easy way to estimate this probability using classical techniques (a Bayesian approach might be more fruitful). However, it seems intuitively plausible that if the urn is well mixed and if we were careful to reach into diverse parts of the urn (matters of judgment), and if green beads are 10% or more of the contents, then at least *one* green bead is going to show up in our handfuls. In other words, if our judgment is good, a judgment sample is going to be perfectly adequate for discovering that "there are some green beads present." If we already know about green beads (and don't care to learn about whether they are tinted a blue green or more of a yellow green), then we wasted our time doing qualitative research focused on color identification. If we had only heard rumors of bead colors other than white, black, and blue, then the opportunity to examine a green bead may have been quite worthwhile. This is why qualitative research is properly used for exploration, but ceases to be very useful when we are seeking confirmation.

In summary, the first argument in favor of the adequacy of judgment samples for qualitative research is that in real-world contexts, good judgment is possible, even expected, and that identity generalization is a relatively forgiving kind of inference (compared with incidence generalization). The second argument for the adequacy of judgment samples is the known inadequacy of probability samples when samples are small. More exactly, the same calculations that allow us to estimate how big a probability sample we require in order to have a good, tight margin of error (i.e., a precise estimate of incidence) indicates that were we to draw a probability sample of four beads, or 16 beads (typical of the number of focus groups or customer visits conducted), and were green beads to be about 10% of those in the urn, then we can be confident that a considerable proportion of those samples of four or 24 would contain *no* green beads. Random means . . . random, the absence of judgment. Thus, the known risks and imprecision of probability samples when sample size is small also supports the use of judgment samples in qualitative research (since the expense of long duration qualitative interviews tends to hold the number of interviews undertaken to a small number, small enough that a probability sample will often miss factors of interest).

The Importance of Understanding the Different Types of Samples

Survey research and most other quantitative research must use probability samples if they are to fulfill their promise to yield precise and projectable estimates of the incidence or level of some item or value in the population. If a probability sample cannot be obtained, particularly in the case of survey research, then it may be premature at best, and a waste of time and money at worst, to undertake quantitative market research at all. By contrast, judgment samples are generally adequate for purposes of qualitative research, as long as there is reason to believe that good judgment is available, and provided that the users of qualitative research restrict their interpretation of results to identity generalizations, and avoid attempting to make incidence generalizations.

Estimating the Required Sample Size

Given a probability sample, estimating how big a sample to draw is quite straightforward, provided that three pieces of information are available:

1. The decision maker's desired margin of error (i.e., degree of precision)

2. The confidence level required

3. The variance, in the population, of the quantity being estimated via the research

The first item is the easiest to explain. Decision makers have to be apprised of the fact that market research conducted using samples of human beings yields only approximate values, that these values (the research results) can be made more or less approximate, that it costs money to make these approximations tighter, and that very tight approximations can cost an order of magnitude more than looser but still serviceable approximations. As an example of a looser but still serviceable approximation, consider a survey that contains a set of opinion statements with which customers have to agree or disagree. Our goal is to identify which opinions, if any, are held by a majority of customers— especially those held by a large majority. Under these circumstances, a decision maker might be satisfied with a margin of error of ±10 percentage points. Thus, if 61% of the customers in the survey agreed with a viewpoint, one could be confident that this view was held by a majority of customers (between 51% and 71%, specifically); if upward of 77% agreed, then one could be confident this view was held by two thirds or more of customers (specifically, 67% to 87%); and if a viewpoint was agreed to by 50%, then one could be confident that it was probably not held by a strong majority (with the degree of adherence in the population estimated at 40% to 60%, given the margin of error of ±10%).

The desired degree of precision (another name for margin of error) is discretionary to the decision maker, and should be matched to the decision at hand. Thus we can envision an alternative scenario, where a corporate goal had been set to improve product documentation and design such that fewer than 20% of customers would suffer from unscheduled downtime within any given three-month period. Large bonuses will accrue if the goal is met; pay raises will be frozen if it is not. Here a much higher degree of precision might be sought, perhaps as few as two percentage points, along with a higher level of confidence, to boot. The sample in this case may have to be 10 or even 100 times as large as in the previous example, given that decision makers might well desire a very tight margin of error in this case.

The next two terms require a brief discussion of statistical theory and usage. Confidence level, more properly *confidence interval*, has a specific meaning in statistics. Although it can be any percentage, it is conventional to use the 95% confidence interval in social science research, corresponding to a significance level of $p = .05$. (See Chapter 11 for more on significance tests.) You will also encounter 90% confidence intervals and 99% confidence intervals, corresponding to significance levels of $p = .10$ and $p = .01$; however, most other values (any value between about 0% and 100% can be estimated) do not appear in practical contexts. To return to the examples explaining margin of error, technically speaking, when we estimate that 61% of customers, ±10%, agree with a viewpoint, we are stating only that if the survey were repeated an infinite number of times, with this same population of customers, then 95% of the time the estimate of the proportion of customers agreeing with this viewpoint will be a value that falls between 51% and 71%.

Put another way, when we say that a given survey has a precision of ±10 percentage points, (or ±3 points, the value typically found in newspaper reports describing Gallup polls taken during election years), we really mean that we are about this much confident (90%, 95%, 99%) that we have obtained the claimed degree of precision. Precision, in samples, is never absolute, but is always precision-at-the-specified-confidence-level. Those readers with the soul of an engineer are free to frown: yes, the precision of our estimates, in quantitative market research, is itself only an estimate. Welcome to research with human beings. Remember what I said in the beginning about market research never eliminating uncertainty, but only reducing it?

The third piece of information we must supply is the variance, in the population, of the quantity we seek to estimate in the sample. *Variance* is a statistical term close in meaning to "variability"; what follows is limited to an intuitive explanation of the concept of variance, and of its importance in determining sample size. It may be helpful to use stock prices as an example. Consider two stocks, one a young speculative Internet stock, like eBay, and the other an old, conservative stock like IBM. Let us further suppose that their average price during the year was about the same, maybe $80 a share or so. Now consider the set of all prices that eBay and IBM may have traded at during this calendar year. We would expect that eBay would have traded at a wider range of prices over the year, relative to its average price in that year, than IBM. In that case, eBay's price series would have a higher measured variance. Now suppose your task was to estimate the average price that eBay or IBM sold for during that year. The only info available is a scattered selection of old newspapers.

The idea connecting variance to sample size estimation is simply that it would be more difficult to estimate the average price of eBay using only a few newspapers; put another way, you would need to sample a greater number of old newspapers in the case of eBay than IBM in order to come close to estimating the average price. In a nutshell this is why you need to estimate the population variance when computing required sample size—the larger the variance, the larger the sample size required to secure a given margin of error.

Formula for Computing Sample Size

Assuming that the population from which we are sampling is much larger than the sample itself, the formula is as follows:

1. Square the Z value associated with the desired confidence interval

2. Multiply it by the population variance

3. Divide by the square of the desired precision.

Precision is the number following the $\pm$ sign in the examples that discussed margin of error. Thus, if our margin of error is ±10 percentage points, the quantity that must be squared to obtain the denominator is .10. If we want to know the average amount spent on music downloads per month, to $\pm\$5$, then 5 is the quantity to be squared. Variance is as just defined; we'll examine how to calculate a numerical value for variance in a minute. The value for the confidence interval, Z, is found in tables showing the area under the curve for normally distributed data ("bell curve"). For our purposes, it is enough to keep the following three Z values in mind:

Z for a 99% confidence interval = ~2.6

Z for a 95% confidence interval = ~2.0

Z for a 90% confidence interval = ~1.6

Here is a simple calculation to anchor the formula. Suppose we are looking at the opinion survey used earlier. Let the margin of error be ±10%; let the chosen confidence interval be 95%; and let the variance for the agree–disagree proportion be .25. The necessary sample size is then computed as follows:

$$2^2 \times .25 \, / \, (.10)^2$$

$$= 4 \times .25 \, / \, .01$$

$$= 100 \text{ customers}$$

If we are correct about the variance associated with these opinion items, then a probability sample of 100 customers will yield results with a precision of ±10 percentage points at the 95% confidence level. Once the three pieces of necessary information are obtained, calculation of the needed sample size is as simple as that.

To empower you to make actual use of this formula, the crucial next step is to explain how to obtain a numerical variance in specific cases. It is straightforward to standardize on the use of the 95% confidence interval, since this is the norm in contemporary social science; departures are sometimes appropriate, but represent exceptions that should be carefully justified. Similarly, decision makers can generally settle on a needed precision after some reflection and coaching. This leaves finding the value of the variance as the major head-scratcher.

Estimating the Variance for a Proportion

This turns out to be the simple case: the variance for a proportion is computed as follows:

$$\text{Variance} = \text{proportion } 1 \times \text{proportion } 2$$

If we are working with agree–disagree items, and we expect that opinion may be evenly split, then the variance to plug into the formula is .50 × .50, or .25, as in the preceding example. Interestingly enough, this is the largest value you will ever have to plug into the formula for the variance of two proportions. For instance, if you expect that customers are opposed to a viewpoint by 2 to 1, then the variance is .666 × .333, or

.22; if you expect an 80–20 split, then the variance is .8 × .2, or .16. Hence, if you don't have any prior expectations about how customer opinion is split, the conservative thing to do is to estimate the needed sample size assuming a 50–50 split. You may end up spending extra money beyond what was needed (should the actual split turn out to be 65–35), but in that event you will achieve extra precision as well.

Estimating the Variance for a Mean Value

Suppose that the survey is aimed at examining numerical values rather than proportions. You may be interested in the average expenditure, the average size of a customer's maintenance budget, the average number of man-hours required by some task, and so forth. Although the formula for computing sample size is the same, estimating the variance requires more information than in the case of proportions. The best approach is to obtain the actual variance, for this question and this population, by examining some previous sample gathered by yourself or someone else. Thus, if this question was used in a trade magazine survey or any secondary research report, the standard deviations may be tabled along with the average values, and the variance may be estimated by squaring the reported standard deviation.

Note that if you are interested in the average customer rating on some rating scale, you can use published values to estimate the variance. Thus the possible variance in numerical terms, for a five-point satisfaction scale, or for a five-point scale indicating the strength of buying intentions, is in each case mostly a function of the fact that there are only five possible ratings that customers can give. This is because variance is computed as the sum of the squared deviations of each value from the population mean, divided by the number of population elements. Because the mean of a set of ratings has a limited range—the largest possible deviation from the mean, given a five-point scale, is about 4—the variance of a rating scale must itself fall within a limited range. The same holds true for any four-point scale, any seven-point sale, and any 10-point scale, regardless of what is being measured. Table 6.1 gives the range of variances typically encountered for commonly used rating scales.

With rating scales, use the lower value in Table 6.1 if you have reason to believe that the distribution of customer responses looks like a

Table 6.1   Estimated Variance for Rating Scales

Number of Scale Points	Example	Variance (Normal Distribution)	Variance (Flat or Skewed Distribution)
4	Performance scale: poor, fair, good, excellent	0.7	1.3
5	Likert scale anchored by strongly agree/strongly disagree with a neutral midpoint	1.2	2.0
7	Semantic differential scale with end points anchored by bipolar opposites (e.g., boring/exciting)	2.5	4.0
10	Ratings of preference or attractiveness	3	7

Note: Use the larger variance to obtain a more conservative estimate of needed sample size, especially if there is considerable uncertainty about the distribution of customer responses.

Adapted from Churchill and Iacobucci (see Chapter 2 Suggested Readings), p. 503.

bell curve, that is, if you expect most customers to give the middle rating, with fewer and fewer customers checking the more and more extreme ratings. If you think checking the distribution will be lopsided, with the majority of customers giving either extremely high or low ratings, or if you think customers will be all over the map, with the middle rating used about as often as the extremes, then use the high value for the variance. Groundwork laid by customer visits and focus groups can be very helpful in making these decisions. Keep in mind also that a precision of, say, ± 0.2 is quite a bit more precise in the case of a 10-point rating scale than in the case of a four-point scale. A desire for tight precision combined with use of a high variance scale (10 points rather than four points) is going to drive sample size, and costs, considerably higher.

Not using a rating scale? No prior research on which to piggyback? A variable like hours per production task, for a complicated manufacturing process, could be very difficult to pin down in advance. (You might even protest, "This sort of ignorance is why we wanted to do research in the first place!") The two possible approaches in such cases are simulation and guesstimation. For purposes of simulation, simply open an Excel spreadsheet and create a plausible distribution for the variable in question, using an assumed sample size that is very small. Thus, using a small sample of 20, your spreadsheet might look like this:

Production Hours Required	Number of Customers at This Level
20	1
25	2
27.5	4
30	6
32.5	4
35	2
40	1
Mean = 30	$N = 20$

You would compute the variance as the sum of the squared deviations from the mean (= 250) divided by the number of population elements (= 20), giving a variance of 12.5. If the decision maker requests a precision of ±1 hour, with a confidence level of 95%, then the needed sample size is $(2^2 \times 12.5)/1 = 50$ factory customers. If you aren't confident that the distribution looks like a bell curve, then flatten it out and recompute the variance (which will be larger), and consider using the larger sample computed thereby, depending on whether the amount at stake justifies a more expensive study.

The guesstimation approach, which is even simpler, takes advantage of that fact that in a normal distribution, 99% of all values will fall within 3 standard deviations of either side of the mean. Here you simply ask yourself, Do I have a feel for the minimum and maximum values I can reasonably expect to encounter? Qualitative research, or plain old industry experience, may indicate that the range of production hours required for the task is probably between 20 and 40. If so, and if normally distributed, then the standard deviation would be the range of 20 divided by 6, or 3.66. Because variance is the square of the standard deviation, you would plug 13.34 into the sample size formula (a result not so different from the variance of 12.5 computed in the Excel spreadsheet simulation, reflecting the fact that the simulation values had the same range and roughly mimicked a normal distribution).

There are doubtless some readers, confronted with these two heuristics, who might reply, "Do I need to spell it out for you: WE HAVEN'T A CLUE! We don't know range or anything else about this value. THAT'S WHY WE WANT TO DO RESEARCH!" Indeed, how do you compute sample size if neither of the heuristics just described seem to apply? The answer is that if you can't even guess the range of some quantity of interest, then it is premature to be doing quantitative research—you need to do some secondary research or qualitative research first. (How could the decision makers even specify the desired precision if they didn't have some sense of the range?) Alternatively, this highly uncertain item may not be central to the research, in which case you can set sample size using information on some other key item, and accept whatever precision that sample size yields for the uncertain item. Precision at a given confidence level can always be calculated after the fact, using the obtained sample size and the obtained distribution of answers, and this precision can be respected in decision making.

Sampling Reminders and Caveats

The first caveat is that the preceding discussion has been drastically simplified relative to any standard statistical treatment of the topic. It would literally take more pages than this chapter itself to list all the assumptions, special cases, and exceptions that have been omitted. If there is a lot of money at stake, you owe it to yourself to consult a statistician experienced in drawing samples. Any competent market research vendor will either have such statisticians on staff or know where to find one. The point to take away is that quantitative research succeeds only to the extent that it is based on good probability samples of adequate size. If the sample is bad or simply too small, a result stated as "a small majority of customers (55%) agreed that . . ." should really be reported as "we won't be too far off if we assume that somewhere between 25% and 85% of our customers would agree that . . ." Precision is everything in quantitative research, and good samples are required if precision is to be adequate.

The second caveat is that the formula for sample size given assumes comparison of a single estimate to some absolute standard—that is, whether more or less than 50% of customers agree with some view. A different formula is required if the task is to determine whether more customers agree with viewpoint A than viewpoint B, or whether customers in segment 1 are more likely to hold viewpoint A than customers in segment 2. The basic approach involving an interplay of confidence level, variance, and precision remains the same, but the formulas used are distinct. Such formulas can be found in market research or other statistical texts under headings such as "Computing Power for a Given Sample Size." The details vary depending on what type of comparison is involved, so professional assistance is advisable.

The third caveat is that precision as discussed in this chapter is precision with respect to random sampling error only. The tacit preface was always "assuming that every other part of the research is free of every other kind of error." Then and only then would a sample of such and such a size have the calculated precision. Because random sampling error is only one of the many kinds of error, it is futile to keep ramping up sample size in search of a vanishingly small margin of error. Other kinds of error (bad sample due to incompetent interviewers, poorly worded questions, inappropriate statistical techniques, etc.) aren't reduced by increases in sample size, and can even be aggravated (as when less competent interviewers are pressed into service to produce a large sample under deadline). Because nonsampling errors are difficult to eliminate (or even detect), large increases in sample size can produce a misleading tightening of precision. Total precision, taking all kinds of error into account, becomes markedly less than the stated precision, which only reflects random sampling error. And it is total precision that matters as far as real-world decisions are concerned.

As a practical matter, commercial studies of proportions should rarely seek a precision any tighter than ±5 percentage points. Similarly, commercial studies of quantities (e.g., production hours) should generally be satisfied with a precision not much tighter than 10% of whatever mean value is expected. If decision makers expect more precision than that, then I suspect they have not really accepted the fact that market research can only reduce uncertainty, not eliminate it.

In terms of reminders, perhaps the most important is that all the calculations in this chapter apply to the final obtained sample, and not to the initial sample. Furthermore, regardless of whether the initial sample was a probability sample, the obtained sample should only be considered a probability sample if nonresponse bias can be judged to be minimal or absent. When response levels are very low, it is difficult to believe that responders are not systematically different from the nonresponders. If a survey doesn't ultimately rest on a probability sample of adequate size, then its results are really no more precise and no more projectable than those of any competently conducted piece of qualitative research.

The second reminder is that sample size really does relate to precision as a matter of mathematical law. If you have an adequately sized probability sample, you are going to achieve a reasonable degree of precision. A corollary is that a sample size of as little as 100 can give more than satisfactory precision in many practical contexts. This is why it can be so powerful and cost-effective to follow up a qualitative research study with a short, focused survey. One hundred phone calls may yield sufficient certainty that a substantial proportion of customers really does hold some negative perception—a perception whose existence went unguessed prior to the discoveries made through qualitative research.

Suggested Readings

Scheaffer, Richard L., William Mendenhall, and Lyman Ott. 1995. *Elementary Survey Sampling*, 5th ed. Boston: Duxbury Press.

> As the title suggests, this text provides an introduction that relies less on advanced mathematics than many other treatments.

Sudman, Seymour. 1976. *Applied Sampling*. New York: Academic Press.

> Addresses the issues involved in determining sample size and selection methods for surveys in marketing and related areas.

7

Survey Research

In survey research, a *questionnaire* is completed by a carefully selected *sample* of respondents. Of course, sample selection is a procedure relevant to all kinds of market research, as discussed in Chapter 6. Similarly, questionnaires may play a role in other kinds of market research. It is thus the conjunction of a certain kind of questionnaire design with a certain approach to sampling that constitutes survey research as a distinct market research tool. Specifically, survey research questionnaires typically seek to describe a person or that person's perceptions, and respondents are sampled with the intention of projecting responses to the larger population from which they were drawn.

A typical example would be a questionnaire delivered to existing customers of a product containing questions concerning customers' global satisfaction with the product, customers' satisfaction with specific aspects of the product, information about the customers themselves, and information about how the product is used. Results of such a survey might be used to assess whether customer satisfaction is above some threshold, and whether it has increased or decreased since the last time it was measured. The results might also be analyzed to see whether some types of customers are more satisfied than others, or to determine whether specific applications of the product seem to increase or decrease overall level of satisfaction.

Surveys as narrowly specified in this chapter may also be termed *descriptive surveys*. The typical result takes the form of a percentage figure (e.g., "35% of home computer users are dissatisfied with their online service provider"), a frequency count (e.g., "on average C++ programmers make two calls per month to software vendors' technical support lines") or a cross-tabulation comparing groups (e.g., "47% of MIS directors with exclusively IBM mainframes reacted favorably to this proposal, as compared to 28% of MIS directors having both IBM and non-IBM mainframes in their shop").

Surveys can be administered in person (somewhat rare today, except for mall intercepts, where a shopper is stopped by a clipboard-toting interviewer), by telephone (still the most common method in commercial market research, although Internet surveys are coming up fast), by mail (not uncommon, but not preferred), and by electronic means (typically taking the form of an E-mail invitation or pop-up that leads the willing respondent to a Web site where the survey resides). Each method of survey administration has its own body of craft knowledge associated with it. Thus, design and execution of a computer-assisted telephone interview draw on a different skill set than design and execution of an Internet-based survey. In keeping with this book's pledge to provide a concise introduction, this chapter steers clear of concepts specific to one or another method of survey administration and concentrates on generally applicable procedures.

The one distinction among methods of administration worth noting here is that interviewer-delivered methods (in person, phone) can be longer and involve more difficult questions (because interviewers have some ability to motivate continued participation and to assist respondents). Interviewer-assisted methods can also handle more complex branching; whereas a print questionnaire must instruct a respondent to skip to question X if the answer to a current question is no, interviewers can execute that skip themselves, with fewer errors, and less potential for discombobulating the respondent. Finally, Internet-based survey administration is growing in popularity because it is both cheap and efficient (no need for a staff of phone interviewers, plus the data are automatically compiled in a spreadsheet, ready for analysis), and perhaps because the approach still retains some novelty value in the eyes of respondents, so that response rates are a little higher than they might otherwise be.

The survey is probably the most familiar of all market research methodologies. Virtually every adult reading this book will have been on the receiving end of some kind of survey: a phone call at home, a letter in the mail, a person with a clipboard in a mall. Moreover, it is a rare business student today who completes an undergraduate or graduate degree in business without having occasion to design, conduct, and analyze at least one survey. This familiarity, combined with the incredible ease with which a survey (especially a bad survey) can be initiated and completed, and in conjunction with the comfort that comes from obtaining seemingly precise numerical data, creates a problem: *there are almost certainly too many surveys being done in market research today!* By this I mean that some substantial portion of the effort business firms currently put into surveys would be more productive if invested instead in either choice-modeling and controlled experiments, on the one hand, or customer visits and focus groups, on the other. In fact, for the managerial reader of this chapter, I would be quite happy if it served as a bucket of cold water. Surveys can be enormously expensive, and if this chapter causes you to question whether your current level of expenditure on surveys is ill-considered, then it has partly served its purpose. The number of cases in business where it is worthwhile to spend a substantial amount of money in order to estimate precisely some percentage or frequency, for primarily descriptive purposes, is limited. If such descriptive precision is really your goal, then of course the survey is the tool of choice; when it is not, then the survey may be a poor use of resources indeed.

The final thing to remember about survey research is that everything depends on the quality of the questionnaire and the effectiveness of the sampling procedure. Surveys, like the other quantitative techniques discussed in subsequent chapters, are in some meaningful sense less robust than the qualitative techniques (customer visits, focus group). Thus, if the initial set of questions prepared for a customer visit study is flawed, new questions and good follow-up questions can be devised in real time as the interviews proceed. With a survey, questions cannot be changed in midsurvey, and we cannot interact with the respondents to clarify their answers. Similarly, although better and worse sampling strategies can be devised for any qualitative research study, the kinds of generalization undertaken with qualitative data (see Chapter 6) are more forgiving of problems with the sample. By contrast, with a survey we are trying to say that the proportion of satisfied customers in this market segment is precisely 35%, with only a small allowance for error. Unless our sample is very good, the number 35% obtained from the statistical output may really only mean "at least 10%, and probably not more than 65% of customers." If accurate description is the goal, such imprecision is disastrous.

To conclude on this same pessimistic note, I would argue that the proportion of surveys conducted by businesspeople that are bad (useless or misleading) is much higher than the proportion of customer visits, focus groups, conjoint analyses, and experiments that are bad in that same sense. More often than not, the problem lies with sampling (arguably, questionnaire design is not as difficult as executing an effective sampling plan). And more often than not, the sampling problem does not lie with the sample that was asked to complete the questionnaire, but with the sample of respondents that actually did complete the questionnaire. If this is 10%, as is often the case with commercially fielded mail questionnaires, it seems unlikely that one has in fact obtained a good sample with respect to precisely describing the population of interest.

Bad surveys not attributable to flaws in the questionnaire or the sample generally result from a failure on the part of the decision maker to justify the need for precise descriptive data. As we will see in Chapters 9 and 10, it is often possible, for an equal or smaller expenditure, to obtain powerful *predictive* data. Most decision makers would prefer good prediction over an accurate description, because such data are more actionable. The prediction is also generally more relevant to deciding among options. If one is in learner mode, descriptive data might be quite interesting (and prediction, premature). But if one is in learner mode, will you learn most by gathering precise descriptive data, or by exploring in depth via qualitative research?

In short, it is difficult to succeed in obtaining a high-quality descriptive survey, and even when you succeed, the accurate descriptions so obtained may not be worth much. Keep this perspective in mind next time someone in your group casually suggests, "Let's send them a survey."

Procedure

It is quite possible (although not always advisable) to conduct a survey yourself; alternatively, you can hire a vendor to do it for you. Survey research is a mainstay of many market research firms and there is no shortage of assistance available. Whereas focus groups are something of a specialty item, and choice modeling even more so, virtually every market research vendor, large or small, conducts surveys. In what follows, the procedure for conducting a survey with a vendor's help is described. Issues involved in conducting your own survey are summarized in the next section.

1. You prepare a request for proposals (RFP) that outlines the characteristics of the population you want to survey (e.g., female heads of

household who own cellular phones), the kinds of information you want to obtain, and the purpose of gathering this information (e.g., to describe current patterns of usage of cellular phones so as to prepare for the design of new calling plans targeted at this population). In the RFP you should also give some indication of the desired sample size and the source of the sample (a list provided by you, a list bought by the vendor, a random calling procedure, etc.), as these are important cost factors. Alternatively, as part of their proposal, vendors may propose solutions to these issues based on their expertise.

You will also have to indicate in the RFP how the survey is to be administered. The default choice is the telephone: it's quicker, it's cost-effective, and it has a much higher response rate than mail administration. However, there are some situations that may require an Internet questionnaire, as when questions are lengthy, complex, or numerous, or require visual stimuli. People can process much greater amounts of information and more complex information by reading as opposed to listening, and if your survey has that kind of complexity, then Internet administration (or as a last resort, administration by paper mail) may be a superior approach. Do ask your vendor for advice on this point.

2. The selected vendor will work with you to hammer out the text of the questions and the answer categories to be used in the survey. See the next chapter for detailed advice on this step.

3. You and the vendor decide upon the size and the source of the sample. As we saw in the preceding chapter, there is no mystery to setting sample size; well-accepted statistical formulas exist. However, these formulas work best when you can provide some prior information to the vendor, such as the expected frequency of different answers. Your vendor will also probably have rules of thumb about sample size based on past experience with surveys of this type. Remember that it is your prerogative as the paying customer to ask for an explanation of how sample size was determined. If you get an evasive answer, or you can't understand the answer, that's a bad sign. The mathematics of sample size selection is straightforward and should be well within your vendor's competence.

The source of the sample is generally a list that you provide, a list that the vendor buys, or some kind of random sampling process, such as random-digit dialing. In random-digit dialing, phone numbers to be called are generated by a computer. The process of number generation anticipates and allows for a fair number of dud calls (businesses, numbers not in service, etc.). The rationale for random-digit dialing is that many people have unlisted phone numbers, and people with unlisted numbers may differ in significant ways from those with listed numbers. Plus, a preexisting list cannot always be found.

The audience for this book—business-to-business and technology firms—is less likely to use random-digit dialing, which is primarily important in mass consumer markets. Instead, you will almost always be working from some kind of list. If you can supply the list, and if it is a good list in the sense of having few duds (i.e., names of people who have moved, changed jobs, don't fit the population), then the cost of your survey research will be substantially less. If the vendor has to buy multiple lists, or if there are no good lists available, then the cost goes up accordingly. The list industry is huge and growing, and some kind of list can generally be obtained, but cost goes up with the rarity and inaccessibility of the sample sought.

The most important thing to remember is that your entire survey research project is only as good as the sample, and that sample is only as good as the list from which it was drawn. If the list is biased—not representative of the population of interest—then your results will be biased as well. For example, suppose you use warranty cards to compile a list. Unfortunately, return rates for warranty cards are notoriously low—5% to 10% in many cases. Who knows how different the nonreturnees may be? Similarly, you may have a list of names of people who attended an industry conference. Some possible problems here include a geographical bias (depending on conference location), an employer success bias (only companies healthy enough to have adequate travel funds sent people to the conference), and so forth. "Know your list" is the rule, and be sure to keep its limits and shortcomings in mind as you analyze results.

4. Next, you pretest the survey. I cannot overemphasize the importance of this step. In any substantial effort you should plan on a small-scale administration to a few dozen members of the target population. After each person completes the survey they are interviewed about possible misunderstandings, the meaning of their answers, and sources of confusion. A survey that may seem perfectly clear to a 38-year-old MBA-educated project manager immersed in the product category may be regarded very differently by a 24-year-old engineer who only uses the product on an occasional basis.

In real-world situations you will often be tempted to skip the pretest because of time pressures. This is yet another example of how it is easier to do a bad survey than a good one. But remember: If the questions on the survey are confusing, if the list of answer categories is incomplete, or if the language is wrong, then it doesn't matter that you have a large, representative sample—your results are still all too likely to approximate garbage. At the very least, ask your spouse and the spouses of teammates to look it over. Get *some* outside minds involved, even if it's only a half dozen.

5. The survey is administered. If it's a telephone survey, computer-assisted telephone interviewing (CATI) will probably be used. The interviewer sits in front of a computer that flashes the questions on the screen and allows the interviewer to enter the answers directly into the tabulation and analysis software. The efficiency of such a procedure is obvious, and one of the reasons that telephone interviewing is preferred is that this automatic tabulation of answers speeds up the analysis and reporting cycle considerably. On the other hand, if it is a mail survey, then there will be an initial mailing followed by a postcard reminder and sometimes one or more follow-up mailings. One of the reasons mail surveys are less preferred is the amount of time consumed by this process, combined with the low response rates (often 10% or less) that typically occur even with several reminders and follow-ups. Internet surveys allow respondents to read questions, as in mail surveys, but automatically record results, as in CATI procedures. As the bulk of the literate population acquires Internet access, the mail questionnaire may well disappear from commercial market research.

6. Next the survey results are analyzed and reported. Typically the basic form of the analysis will be a comprehensive breakout of the frequency of the answers to each question on the survey. For example, if the question was, "Do you use your computer for any of the following applications?," the report might then include a chart showing:

PERCENTAGE USING APPLICATION

63% word processing

35% spreadsheets

29% communications

28% graphics

20% games

37% other

If the question had been, "How satisfied are you with each aspect of your computer, using a scale where 10 equals 'completely satisfied' and 1 equals 'not satisfied at all'?," the results might look like this:

AVERAGE PERFORMANCE RATINGS, DELL PC OWNERS

7.5 performance

8.2 color graphics

6.0 expandability

5.7 preloaded software

7.9 reliability

Most reports also include a number of cross-tabulations that combine answers to two or more questions. For instance, you might want to compare the applications typically used by owners of IBM PCs to those typically used by owners of Apple Macintoshes. Then you would see a chart something like this:

	PC Owners (n = 893)	Macintosh Owners (n = 102)
Word processing	70%	48%
Spreadsheets	49%	22%
Communications	27%	30%
Graphics	12%	58%
Games	15%	31%

A good report includes a variety of additional data. In an appendix or elsewhere, look for information on confidence intervals (i.e., the precision of the percentages or averages contained in the report). You need to know how many percentage points have to separate two estimates before you can trust that there is a real difference. Thus, in the first example above, with any decent-sized sample we can probably conclude that word processing is a more common application than spreadsheets; but are spreadsheets really any more common than communication applications? There's no easy way to know unless the vendor has included the necessary information on confidence intervals. You must recognize that a survey only gives estimates of the true values in the total population, and any estimate is only that—a probable value. Do not fall into the trap of treating the numbers in a survey as an oracular pronouncement or a window onto truth.

Other data whose presence should add to your comfort with the vendor and the survey include information on response rate along with comparisons, to the extent possible, of how respondents differ from nonrespondents. If the response rate is low, your confidence in the results has to be lowered accordingly. For instance, you may have started out with a large, representative sample of technical support employees; but if only 10% of these people returned your survey, then your obtained sample is probably both small in number (making the results less precise) and systematically different from the population of interest—the total population of all technical support personnel in the market you serve. However, if the list you used to obtain the sample contained some additional information beyond name and phone number—for instance, each support person's years of experience and whether they work in hardware or software support—and if you compared people who responded to the survey with people who did not, then you may be able to establish whether or not the obtained sample is biased on these two counts. If in fact the obtained sample of support personnel is similar to the initial sample in terms of years of experience and the hardware/ software split, then your confidence that the sample is representative goes back up, despite the low response rate.

On the other hand, if there is no information that allows a comparison between respondents and nonrespondents, then, as a rule of thumb, the lower the response rate, the less confidence you should have in the results. Large percentage differences in the case of high response rates (i.e., a 62%/38% split on an agree–disagree question where the response rate is 80%) are unlikely to vanish altogether even when there is substantial response bias. The same majority of 62% agreement, but with a response rate of only 20%, will disappear if the nonrespondents happen to split 53% to 47% in the reverse direction. As a general rule of thumb, a small percentage difference (say, 55%/45%) on an agree–disagree question will be virtually uninterpretable in the case of a low response rate. It could easily be the opposite of the true breakdown of responses in the population at large.

Conducting the Survey Yourself

If you have another department within your firm conduct the survey (your in-house market research staff, for instance), then this section does not apply—that's not much different than retaining an outside specialist. In this section I am concerned with you—the generalist—doing the survey yourself. Conducting your own survey is probably a bad idea if any of the following conditions hold true:

1. Major decisions will rest on the data obtained.
2. It's a lengthy survey designed to capture a great deal of information.
3. You want a large, high-quality sample to complete the survey.
4. You intend to conduct elaborate analyses of the data.

If the decision is that important, why would you not be willing to obtain the expertise of a skilled professional? Parts of survey research, especially conducting the interviews and tabulating and analyzing the replies, can be very labor intensive and time-consuming. Is it that you or your employees have idle time that you want to put to good use? (Hah!) Moreover, writing a good questionnaire, defining a good sample, conducting the survey in an unbiased manner, and correctly analyzing the results are all specialized technical skills unlikely to be possessed by the typical product, project, or program manager.

By contrast, you probably can effectively conduct your own survey under the following circumstances:

1. The decision, while not unimportant, cannot justify a substantial expenditure.
2. You have a few straightforward questions and a couple of issues that you want clarified.
3. You would be content so long as the sample is not awful, or you have a captive sample, or you can take a virtual census of the relevant population.
4. The goal of your analysis is to identify lopsided majorities or split opinions via simple tabulations.

These circumstances are not uncommon. Maybe you want to ask a few questions of your field sales force, and their management has agreed to assist you. Maybe you have customers attending an event and you are curious about a couple of things. Of course you should have some kind of warranty card included with your product and of course this card should include a couple of questions. If you don't take any one instance of this kind of survey too seriously, and if you keep each such survey short and simple, and you do these surveys as one part of your information gathering, then yes, it makes sense to do these surveys, and yes, you can do them yourself.

You should ask yourself several questions, however. First, will the survey really make any difference? What will you do with the data that you couldn't do without it? Any survey requires a chunk of your time— precious time of which you have too little. Second, how would your time be better spent: searching for high-quality secondary research, or conducting a not-great, not-awful survey yourself? This has to be answered on a case-by-case basis. If no relevant or useful secondary data exists, then of course you may have no choice but to do your own survey. But it would be a shame if you labored mightily to produce an okay survey when in fact there existed some outstanding secondary research that you could have found if only you had gone to the trouble. Third, are you seeking a *description,* or some *understanding?* If the latter, why not make a series of semistructured phone calls (a kind of customer visit), as opposed to firing off a written survey. A semistructured phone interview really isn't a survey because it has so much flexibility. You're not calling to take a count, but to get inside people's heads and gain a perspective. That's an interview, not a survey. In which case, you want a few starter questions, but you want the emphasis in the phone call to be on the follow-up questions that you formulate on the spot in response to what the person said. As noted in Chapter 4, and in contrast to survey research, you are probably better placed than an outside vendor to conduct an effective interview. So why not do what you do best?

Cost Factors

Sample size. Small samples of about 100 can often be professionally surveyed for less than $10,000. Larger samples of 1,000 or more can drive the cost to well over $100,000, $250,000, or more, depending on sample size. (Of course, it can be quite inexpensive to obtain a sample of 1,000, if you begin with an E-mail to 375,000 people; but how much confidence in the representativeness of the results can there be when the response rate is less than 1%?)

Sample accessibility. If lists of these people are expensive, or if the lists are bad so that many calls are wasted, or if these people are hard to reach on the phone, or if many refuse to participate, or if many terminate the interview prior to completion, then the cost goes up accordingly.

Survey length. Phone surveys that require 5 to 10 minutes to complete can be quite inexpensive. As length increases, the cost goes up even faster. Forty-five minutes is probably the maximum feasible for a phone interview, and perhaps 12 pages for a mail questionnaire; less than 20 minutes and four pages are good targets to strive for.

Analysis. If you want many cross-tabulations, or more sophisticated statistical analyses, or more elaborate reporting, then the cost increases. However, analysis costs are generally modest relative to the three factors named above.

Examples

Because surveys are such a familiar kind of research, this section describes a range of applications rather than giving one or two specific case studies. Although the survey is an enormously flexible tool, the eight applications described below probably account for the bulk of the market research surveys conducted in a given year.

Customer satisfaction. In a customer satisfaction survey, a large and representative sample of a firm's customers will be telephoned and asked to rate the firm's performance in a variety of areas. These may include relatively specific actions (e.g., "timely response to inquiries") and more general and intangible aspects (e.g., "offers solutions that are at the cutting edge of the industry"). Customers may also be asked to indicate whether or not certain problems have occurred (e.g., "Has your system required a service call?"). Customers give their ratings on 10-point scales or similar measures. The primary output of this survey will be numerical indices that report, in both global and specific terms, how well the firm is doing. These satisfaction surveys will typically be repeated on a quarterly, semiannual, or annual basis so that trends can be discerned.

Segmentation studies. In a segmentation survey a large and inclusive sample of customers for some product or service will be asked a wide variety of questions. For example, some years ago Levi Strauss conducted a survey to segment the market for men's clothing. Attitude questions (e.g., "Dressing right is a complete mystery to me"), shopping behaviors (e.g., "Do you prefer to shop on your own or with someone else?"), and usage data (e.g., "How many suits do you own?"), were determined. The goal in a segmentation survey is to gather enough data that well-defined clusters of consumers with distinct buying preferences can be identified. In the Levi Strauss study, the "classic independent" segment emerged as the best target market for wool-blend clothing, as compared with some of the other segments (e.g., "mainstream traditionalists"), for whom a different product (polyester suits) was more attractive. The primary goal of a segmentation survey is to provide a rich description of the differences among groups of consumers, along with linkages between these differences and behaviors of interest (heavy usage, brand preference, etc.). Complex multivariate statistical analyses can be performed to produce a pictorial representation of segment differences and preferences.

Product usage and ownership. In the case of innovative product categories, it is often of interest to know what kinds of people have adopted a product early in its life cycle, what they use it for, and what other products are used with it. For instance (this example was current in 2004), what kinds of people have bought an MP3 music player? How many songs do they have stored on it? What proportion of songs came from Internet downloads, versus the proportion ripped from purchased CDs? Even mundane and noninnovative products may benefit from a usage survey if years have passed since the last survey. A bank might survey its customers on which bank products are used (checking, savings, certificates of deposit, etc.), by whom, how heavily, and for what purpose. The primary goal in any product usage survey is to get more complete and detailed information on product users and nonusers, or heavy versus light users, so as to facilitate subsequent marketing, advertising, and product development efforts.

Purchase intentions. A purchase intentions survey examines how many of which kind of people intend to buy some product or service within the next 6 to 12 months. Sometimes these questions are combined with a product usage survey. The primary goal in a product intentions survey is to get data useful for forecasting future sales.

Brand image and perceptions. In a brand image survey, you try to understand how your brand is regarded in the marketplace (often in comparison with other brands). Most often questions will take the form of rating scales ("On a scale of 1 to 5, how prestigious is this brand?"), and the factors rated can range from very tangible to very intangible ("provides good value" versus "daring" or "mainstream"). Whereas a satisfaction survey is primarily evaluative—a kind of report card—a brand image survey is primarily descriptive—a profile or portrait. The goal in a brand image survey is typically either to more broadly diagnose problems (in the case of a brand that has lost ground in a market) or to diagnose strengths and weaknesses (often in preparation for a new advertising campaign).

Tracking studies. Advertisers use tracking studies to determine whether an ad campaign is having the desired effect. The typical procedure is to conduct a baseline survey prior to the launch of the ad campaign. The survey may measure brand awareness, brand image, knowledge of a brand's features and capabilities, usage type or frequency, or anything else that the advertising campaign is aimed at changing. At regular intervals following the launch of the campaign, this survey will be readministered to a new sample drawn so as to be comparable to the baseline sample. The primary goal of a tracking study is to determine whether the ad campaign is working and how well. If a tracking study is conducted apart from any ad campaign, then its purpose is probably trend monitoring: for instance, how many people are considering purchase of a digital camera, current beliefs about the quality of digital camera photos relative to those taken with a film camera, and so forth. Some of the major advertising agencies conduct such surveys to monitor changes in lifestyles and values.

Media usage. A media usage survey asks about magazines read, television programs watched, preferences in radio format, and the like for some specified group of people (e.g., buyers of a certain product category, such as mutual funds). A media usage study will probably be conducted by the vendor firm or its ad agency in order to guide the allocation of ad spending toward the most efficient media vehicles. Thus, you may discover that a large number of networking engineers happen to read *Scientific American* magazine, and that the ad rates in this magazine compare favorably with those of more obvious choices such as *PC Magazine*. Media spending is so substantial (Intel has spent hundreds of millions of dollars promoting its brand of processor chips, and Procter and Gamble spends over a billion dollars per year) that even a quite expensive media survey may quickly pay for itself if it leads to a marginally better allocation of media dollars.

Readership studies. A readership survey will be conducted by a magazine or other media vehicle in order to develop a profile of the people who read the magazine. Readers are the "product" that magazines sell to advertisers, who are their true customers (advertising dollars account for the bulk of magazine revenues). The readership questionnaire asks demographic (age, occupation, income, etc.), psychographic (attitudes, opinions, interests, hobbies, lifestyle), and product usage questions. The primary goal is to describe the readership so as to facilitate efforts to market the magazine to advertisers. If you are a provider of instructional software aimed at children, and if I can show you that my readers are very interested in education and child development, and have substantial discretionary spending power, then I can hope to win some of your advertising dollars.

Strengths and Weaknesses

The great strength of survey research is its ability to deliver precise numerical estimates of the frequency and magnitude of some consumer response. Survey research tells us not that "many" customers are seeking some benefit, but that 39% desire it; not that satisfaction has "decreased," but that satisfaction has dropped from 8.6 to 7.8 on a 10-point scale; not that new computer owners "regularly" purchase software, but that owners spend an average of $586 on software in the year following purchase. This strength is valuable because ultimately most businesses have to measure their success in precise numerical terms: profit dollars, unit sales, market share percentage. In turn, survey research is most useful to businesses in situations where precision matters a great deal, that is, where small differences can be consequential. Thus, any percentage that ultimately concerns the potential size or growth of your market had better be precise. A few percentage points may translate to tens of millions of dollars and may mean the difference between a market big enough to be worth pursuing or too small to consider entering. Similarly, precision is valuable when a high level of uncertainty would be intolerable. Thus, you could conduct lengthy visits with dozens of customers, hear all kinds of stories about your product, and still have no clear sense of whether the overall satisfaction of your customer base is increasing, staying level, or dropping. In any application that requires or resembles a scorecard, a forecast, or a comparison of magnitudes, the precision of survey research will be valuable.

A second strength of survey research lies in its superior objectivity—its capacity to break you free of biases. Businesspeople are continually creating and revising a mental map that describes their customers, competition, and markets, and all kinds of daily experiences feed into that map. Unfortunately, because virtually all businesses have to deal with markets that range in size from large to huge to gigantic to vast, the personal experience of each businessperson is necessarily limited and partial, and thus biased to some unknown degree. Just as an automobile extends the legs, and a telescope the eyes, a good survey extends personal inquiry. Your questions are put to a much larger number of people than you could personally interview, and this large number (in a good survey) represents that still larger population of customers that constitutes your market. Thus, the survey can be thought of as a "question machine" that, like all machines, functions to expand unaided human capacity.

In a sense the amplification capacity of the survey, its ability to extend your individual effort, actually functions to correct two kinds of biases: those due to personal *prejudice,* and those due to personal *limitations.* That is, as individuals we all have personal viewpoints that shape our perceptions. These viewpoints accommodate our individual experience—most notably, the angry customer we spoke to yesterday, the sales pitch that works for us, the friendly customer who always takes our phone calls, and so forth. Unfortunately, no individual is large enough to directly encounter all the diverse components of an entire market. Of course, objectivity, like precision, matters most when you face a close call and some evidence exists in favor of both options. Here the survey functions as the equivalent of a microscope, clarifying a difference too small to be reliably discriminated based on the personal experiences of you and your debating partners.

A third strength of survey research is that it allows you to apply a wealth of statistical techniques that can enhance the rigor and add to the depth of your knowledge. An enormous amount of academic research, developed over a period of 50 years or more, has been directed at developing tools for analyzing the kind of data that surveys produce. Although such narrowly focused and arcane academic research is sometimes the butt of jokes in practical business circles, let me suggest that statistical analysis is like the police—it's easy to have a dismissive attitude until the day your need is acute. How big is "big"? How precise is "precise"? How different is "different"? It is the purpose of statistical analysis to answer such questions, and when millions of dollars hang on getting the right answer, you may come to appreciate the many ways in which survey research lends itself to analysis in statistical terms.

Another strength of surveys is their capacity for illuminating and pinning down differences between groups. A large sample and a precise estimate enable you to do two things: first, to determine whether a difference between groups really exists, and second, to more accurately describe the nature of any difference that does exist. Intergroup comparisons are typically important in segmentation analysis and in the assessment of strengths and weaknesses relative to the competition. For instance, suppose you find that your customers are on average working in larger facilities and concentrated in Sunbelt states, as compared with your competition. That knowledge will make your marketing efforts more effective. For another example, exactly how do people who prefer to put their savings in certificates of deposit differ from those who prefer to put their savings in money market mutual funds—in terms of education, income, source of savings, and geographical region? That knowledge can make your advertising appeals stronger. Again, small differences may have a major dollar impact in terms of the efficiency of marketing and advertising efforts, and an effective survey research procedure may be the only way to uncover such differences.

Lastly, surveys become especially powerful when they are repeated over time. There are a couple of reasons why repeating a survey at intervals is often money well spent. First, most markets are dynamic rather than static. Repeated surveys thus yield data on trends. Furthermore, actually possessing data from multiple past points in time probably provides a more accurate picture of the evolution of a market than asking customers to give a retrospective account of how things have changed over the past few years. Similarly, for forecasting purposes you are better off projecting a trend from several data points than trying to take a single data point (i.e., the customer's self-forecast) and extrapolate it.

From another angle, when a survey is repeated many small biases that may bedevil a single administration cancel out. Thus, the estimate of brand awareness you took today may be off the mark because your sample is a biased subset of the population. But if you use the same questions and sampling procedure three or four times, and the data show an upward trend, that trend is probably more reliable than the absolute value (i.e., 20% or 24%) that you estimated in any single administration.

Perhaps the most significant weakness of descriptive survey research is that it tends to tell you *what* but not *why*. You learn that customer satisfaction is down but you don't know why. You find out that a substantial percentage of your customers are interested in a piece of functionality but you don't learn what is driving that interest. Of course, this is not a problem if you combine the survey with more exploratory techniques such as focus groups or customer visits. It is a big problem if you expect to do only survey research for your market research effort.

A related but more subtle weakness is that typically a survey cannot reveal what you didn't know you didn't know. If you *do* know what it is that you don't know, then you can devise the questions and the answer categories needed to resolve that uncertainty. Thus, surveys can readily answer a question such as, "Which of these problems is most commonly experienced by our customers?" However, surveys aren't very good at answering questions such as, "What new and unexpected problems have begun to bother our customers?" This is because surveys emphasize closed-ended questions in which the answer categories are prespecified rather than open-ended questions. In a word, surveys are a precision tool, not a discovery tool.

Another weakness of surveys is that they rely on self-report data. If the customer does not know something, or cannot or will not verbalize that something, or cannot accurately describe that something, then a survey will not reveal it. Some examples of information you might like to gain but that customers may be unable to self-report include (a) what they will do in the future, (b) what the most important factor is in their purchase decision (they can tell you what they think is important, but will this be reflected in their actual behavior?), (c) what other people in their organization think or do, (d) exactly how much time or money they spent on something, (e) which parts of the user interface cause them to make errors, and so forth. Just as the weaknesses of surveys with respect to explanation and discovery drive you to supplement surveys with focus groups and customer visits, so also the weaknesses associated with self-report data should drive you to supplement descriptive surveys with conjoint analysis and experimentation. In these alternative research techniques people *act* rather than or in addition to *speaking,* and analyses of these actions can reveal matters of which the customer is unaware or that the customer is incapable of verbalizing.

A more subtle weakness of survey research is that most of the time, for most people, participation in a survey is intrinsically unrewarding. This is one reason why phone surveys are more commonly used in market research than mail surveys: it is harder to ignore or dismiss a phone call as opposed to a letter. Surveys are not fun. People participate out of inertia, out of a sense of obligation (recognizing that their information is probably useful), or to give voice (more likely in the case of aggrieved customers, which of course introduces a bias). In comparison to an interview, which is a person-to-person encounter, and which offers potential rewards such as feeling understood, getting through to someone else, learning something, being stimulated to think, enjoying company, and so forth, ultimately, participating in a survey means becoming grist for a statistical mill—an opportunity to be an instance of a population rather than a unique individual. How does that feel to you?

Two implications follow from this weakness. First, surveys tend to be most useful for getting broad but shallow data. You can't ask hard, provocative, challenging questions because respondents won't play. You can't do extensive follow-up on answers because you are not employing phone interviewers with that level of skill (and a mail questionnaire cannot have too many branching paths). Second, surveys have to be designed to minimize the costs of responding and to maximize the rewards (Dillman, 1999). In designing a survey you have to drive toward brevity and ease of responding. Otherwise, the cost goes way up and the quality goes down. If the survey is too taxing, so many people will discontinue taking it that the representativeness of your obtained sample will be called into question.

Yet another weakness, implicit in much of what has been said earlier, is that surveys are only as good as the sample and the questions used. It would be fascinating to study how our society developed to the point where ordinary college-educated people became prone to assume that surveys are clear glass windows onto the truth. The source of this delusion might be the respect paid to quantification, or perhaps the rhetorical power of anything that sounds scientific. Howsoever, from my perspective as someone holding a Ph.D. in social psychology and knowing a smattering of philosophy of science, it is nothing short of appalling how credulous the average businessperson becomes when confronted with a survey. DON'T FALL INTO THIS TRAP! Gazing at a four-color pie chart, the tendency is to say "Wow—63% of the market wants the product to do this—let's build that functionality in!" A more accurate statement would often be,

> "63% of the people we managed to get on the phone, whose names happened to be on the only list we could afford, and who stuck with us to this point in the survey, answered the only question we knew to ask with an indifferent "sure, why not?"

Don't kid yourself that a survey yields truth. Think instead of surveys as yielding one more fallible data point, to be combined with other data that are fallible for different reasons, as input to a decision that ultimately remains your own, but which is more likely to be successful because you gathered diverse kinds of data.

A final weakness of survey research applies mostly to business-to-business markets where the characteristic purchase decision is made by a group rather than an individual. A survey of individuals is unlikely to address the group decision-making process effectively. Even if the total survey includes people holding various job roles, it probably was not designed to include the full set of job roles from each company included in the sample. This is one of the great advantages of on-site customer visits: you can meet with several decision makers at each firm you visit, alone or in groups.

Do's and Don'ts

Don't fall into the trap of assuming that a large sample size can overcome sample bias. True, small samples give unstable results, independent of whether there is systematic bias; but once the sample size is adequate, further doubling or tripling its size does not in any way reduce whatever systematic bias may be present. If your list contains an unusual percentage of chemists with Ph.D.'s, relative to the total population of chemists, then your obtained sample is going to be biased by this high education level, regardless of how big the sample is or how high the response rate might be. Hence, there is no substitute for a good list or sampling procedure.

Do look at confidence intervals on all means and percentages contained in survey reports. Be sure to find out how big the difference between two numbers has to be before you can be confident that that difference is real.

Do conduct focus groups or customer visits in preparation for surveys. Look to these exploratory procedures for information on what topics to include in the surveys, what language to use, what questions to ask, and what answer categories to use.

Do prepare rough tables and table headings for all frequency counts and cross-tabulations you expect to produce in the analysis of the survey. The point of doing this is to see whether you actually have a use for or need of certain questions. The tendency in survey design is to ask lots of questions in the hope that something interesting will emerge. This is a bad idea. When you are forced to rough out table headings in advance, you will find yourself asking in certain cases, "What's the point? What good will this do me?" Whenever you ask that, your next question should be, "Should I even bother with this particular item on the survey?" Often the answer is no.

Don't indulge idle curiosity. The longer the survey, the more it will cost and the more likely the obtained sample will prove to be unrepresentative because of excessive attrition. Every question in the survey should do a job that needs doing. If you can't meet this standard—if your basic feeling is one of overwhelming ignorance or uncertainty, and this is the factor driving you toward the kitchen-sink approach to survey design—then you probably are not ready to conduct a survey. You need to do more secondary research, customer visits, or focus groups.

Do ask managers to predict the results of key questions. Ask them what the major points of difference will be between two groups. Ask them to predict the approximate percentage of agreement and disagreement with certain opinion statements. Get them on the record. The point of doing this is to make it impossible to say, after a survey has been done, "We already knew that," when in fact the results are a surprise. Documenting the fact that survey research yielded a fresh perspective and corrected some misunderstandings is one of the ways that you establish the value of market research.

Do think of the survey in terms of a social exchange between sponsor and respondent. Exchanges are facilitated when you find ways to minimize the perceived cost of the exchange and maximize the perceived benefits. In the case of surveys you minimize the cost by keeping them short and making the questions as clear and easy to answer as possible. You maximize the benefits by making the questions relevant and of obvious importance—things a customer would want a vendor to know about or understand.

References and Suggested Readings

Alreck, Pamela, and Robert Settle. 1994. *Survey Research Handbook,* 2nd ed. New York: McGraw-Hill.

Rossi, Peter H., James D. Wright, and Andy B. Anderson. 1983. *Handbook of Survey Research.* New York: Academic Press.

These two volumes offer comprehensive coverage of topics associated with designing, conducting, and analyzing surveys.

Dillman, Don A. 1999. *Mail and Internet Surveys: The Tailored Design Method,* 2nd ed. New York: Wiley.

One of the best first books to read on survey research. Gives many practical suggestions and focuses on actions required to maximize response.

8

Questionnaire Design

As we saw in the introduction to Chapter 7, *questionnaire* is a broader and more inclusive term than *survey*. A questionnaire may be defined as any fixed set of questions intended to be completed by some group of respondents. The key point is that the set of questions to be asked and the arrangement of those questions is fixed in advance (this is why it is bad form to refer to the discussion guides used in qualitative research as questionnaires; with discussion guides, anything can vary from interview to interview, including the questions that actually get asked, their sequence, their phrasing, etc.). Also central to the idea of a questionnaire is the expectation that it will be administered to a large number of respondents, so that the distribution of answers to any given question is the focus of interest. With a questionnaire, we are generally uninterested in the fact that John Smith gave a "no" answer to question 17. This is because we aren't interested in learning about John Smith the individual; rather, we want to understand the population of which he is a member. If you are developing fixed sets of questions to be completed by individual customers, with the goal of better understanding each individual who answers, it is probably better to refer to these questions as a form, an instrument, documentation, or just paperwork. Job applications, registration forms, and standardized achievement tests all contain fixed sets of questions but are not considered to be questionnaires.

The advice in this chapter concerns only questionnaires as defined above. Unless otherwise noted, I have in mind a questionnaire designed as part of a survey research project. However, much of the advice also applies to other kinds of questionnaires. Nonsurvey applications of the questionnaire would include those used in concept tests (to be discussed in Chapter 10), the evaluation forms often completed by customers after a training session or other event, warranty cards, and so forth. A thread that runs through the chapter is that the customer's completion of the questionnaire is to some degree elective or optional— in other words, a survey questionnaire is typically a document that the customer is quite free to toss in the wastebasket. Hence, the need to motivate the customer to participate, and to complete the questionnaire once begun, becomes an important design criterion.

Procedure

1. Generate a list of potential topics to be covered and the kind of information to be collected. A group session with a white board may be helpful. This session will work best, however, if the team leader brings a short list to serve as a seed. (More information on generating the content for a questionnaire can be found in the next section.)

2. Construct a first draft of the questionnaire. This draft should consist of actual questions and answer categories, in the expected sequence. Lists of topics and categories of information only take you so far; at a relatively early point in the design process, it is important to draft something that looks like a questionnaire, not a bulleted list. Many problems only become evident when one attempts to take the vague "information on their applications for the product" and translate it into specific questions and answer categories. Generally speaking, the project leader undertakes this draft. If there are problems with the scope or thrust of the desired information, these generally become apparent when the initial draft is attempted. Thus, the number of questions required to come even close to covering a topic may prove unacceptably large (this may happen when the topic is better suited to a customer visit or other exploratory techniques). Or a seemingly simple topic might have so many contingencies associated with it as to be unwieldy. What makes questionnaire design difficult is that the questions have to stand on their own; there is little opportunity, even if administered by an interviewer, for someone to assist the customer in grappling with difficult questions (either the phone staff is not sufficiently knowledgeable, or too many heterogeneous, improvised clarifications to the questionnaire make it unlikely that answers can be

meaningfully aggregated). The process of drafting actual questions brings such issues to the fore.

3. As with any creative task, one of the best things for the leader to do, following completion of the first draft, is to put it aside for a few days—at least, overnight, and preferably until later in the week or over the weekend. Then, take another look at the draft. You'll be surprised how many changes often get made on your second attempt at a first draft. The worst thing to do is to complete the first draft, and then immediately attach it to a broad-cast E-mail requesting comments from the team. The most likely outcome of such speedy action is that several of your teammates will decide that you are perhaps not as capable a questionnaire designer as they had hoped.

4. Let me acknowledge that this advice is much easier for a profes-sor to follow than for the typical overburdened manager. However, the poor working conditions that many managers must endure—for that is what they are—don't change this fundamental fact of human cognitive processing: there is a digestion component in any creative activity. When you put aside the questionnaire draft, at least overnight, your total intel-ligence, of which the processes immediately available to the conscious mind are only a part, has the opportunity to go to work on the problem and uncover new perspectives or alternative avenues of attack. In short, the construction of a questionnaire, unlike memos, status reports, and similar appurtenances to bureaucratic life, represents a design process that benefits from being extended over time.

5. Once the team leader is satisfied that the best possible draft has been created, it is now useful to circulate that draft more widely for comments and critique. A meeting may be useful to incorporate or address the comments made by various parties. A reason that group input to the draft questionnaire is so helpful at this point is that any one person designing a questionnaire will have a particular cognitive style and probably some quirks in terms of chosen mode of expression. However, the questionnaire has to succeed in being clear and under-standable across a wide range of respondents with diverse cognitive styles. Having the questionnaire vetted by a group typically uncovers idiosyncratic turns of phrase, or approaches to the subject matter that would fail to be clear to respondents not having the same cognitive style as the questionnaire drafter. In sum, revisions suggested by the team, all other things being equal, serve to make the questionnaire more robust

against misunderstanding. Of course, if the team consists exclusively of graduates of a particular MIT engineering program, this robustness is unlikely to be achieved; but most teams incorporate some diversity.

Another benefit of having a wider group vet the draft is that key omissions are likely to be uncovered—topics at least as pertinent to the research objective as those included, but which for some reason fell into the team leader's blind spot. Similarly, the draft questionnaire will almost always be excessively long. It is useful for the team as a whole to discuss which topics and questions have the lowest priority, to facilitate subsequent editing and shortening.

6. The team leader, or whoever is ultimately responsible for devising the questionnaire, should then retire and create a second draft. If the project is complex, or there is a lot at stake, or the principal parties are relatively new to questionnaire design, then this second draft again should be circulated for comments. Most of the major problems have been resolved by this point, but there may still be many opportunities to improve the phrasing of question stems and answer categories. Plus, there are probably one or two topics where the best approach remains uncertain.

7. After incorporating feedback on the second draft, the questionnaire designer should attempt a penultimate draft. This draft should observe all space constraints, phrasing and sequencing should be in their proposed final form, and interviewer instructions (if it is to be administered by phone or in person) or preparatory material (if it is to be self-administered in print, by mail, or over the Web) should be drafted.

8. In any project where the stakes are substantial, a pretest should now be conducted. A small sample of people from the respondent pool should be enlisted to complete the questionnaire and then discuss their experiences in so doing. Such a pretest serves as a final disaster check and almost always introduces additional clarity at the margin.

9. The final version of the questionnaire is then ready to be administered.

Generating Content for Questionnaires

The preceding section described a process for moving from the blank page to a completed questionnaire. Here we take a closer look at possible sources for the specific questions and answer categories that will make up the questionnaire.

First, revisit your research objectives. Try to translate these in a direct way into topics to be covered in the questionnaire. Thus, if the objective is to describe the process used to qualify new vendors, possible topics include (1) Who plays a role in vendor selection? (2) How is vendor qualification triggered? and (3) How often is the preferred vendor list revised or updated? Similarly, if the objective is to prioritize customer requirements, then the first step is to list the known requirements, and the second step is to decide whether customers will rate the importance of each one, rank order the list from most to least important, and so forth. The point is that if the research objectives have been well chosen, then they should map directly onto the content of the final questionnaire, with topics, or categories of information, serving as the linking term.

Next, review past questionnaires from within and without your organization. The first reason do this is that there is no point in reinventing the wheel. Many of the questions that appear in any one market research questionnaire also appear in countless other market research questionnaires. This is particularly true for background information, assessments of satisfaction, ratings of quality, and the like; countless firms, across the whole spectrum of industries and technologies, ask some version of these questions, over and over. If someone else has already hammered out a serviceable phrasing, customized to fit your industry, then there is no point in starting from scratch. You are still responsible for making an independent judgment as to whether the phrasing and answer categories are suitable (many existing questionnaires are of poor quality), but there is no need to shut yourself away from existing precedents when generating items for a questionnaire (if you wanted to create completely novel questioning approaches, you should have gone into academia, not industry).

The second reason for reviewing prior questionnaires is to ensure that both your questions and your answer categories are consistent with prior data. Given this consistency, many interesting and fruitful comparisons can potentially be drawn between your data and other data. This point is obvious in the case of satisfaction data—one is almost always interested in comparing present satisfaction levels to past levels, and this group's satisfaction level to some other group's level—but it applies to all kinds of questionnaire content. In a sense, you multiply the analytic power and potential of your results whenever you include questions and answer categories that have been used in other questionnaires.

The point applies most strongly to the answer categories. There may be a dozen different ways to phrase a question about global satisfaction with a purchase, all roughly equivalent in meaning. The important thing is whether, for the answer categories, both present and prior questionnaires used a five-point scale labeled only at the extremes with "very satisfied" and "very dissatisfied," or whether one questionnaire instead used a four-point scale, with each step labeled respectively as "completely satisfied," "satisfied," "partially satisfied," and "not satisfied." There is no exact way to equate the distribution of answers to the five-point and four-point scales just described, and hence no way to say whether the satisfaction of the one group of customers measured the one way is greater or lesser than the satisfaction of another group measured the other way. It behooves you to avoid this trap by standardizing on a particular set of answer categories for questions of this sort.

As an aside, there do not seem to be any copyright issues when one copies a single item or set of answer categories from an existing instrument. Even if copyright obtains, it would generally apply to the questionnaire in its entirety, and only with respect to exact duplications of it. Moreover, the owner of the prior questionnaire would have difficulty showing that no one else had ever asked the question that way (imagine attempting to assert a copyright on either of the satisfaction answer scales just described). Of course, I am not qualified to give legal advice, and if you are duplicating a substantial proportion of what is clearly someone else's unique efforts, then you may wish to consult an attorney knowledgeable in matters of intellectual property.

The next step is to consult textbooks on market research, survey research, and questionnaire design. Most such sources contain many examples of different approaches to asking and answering the basic questions that appear over and over in market research.

Last, the ultimate source of questionnaire content is of course your own background knowledge and ingenuity. The more time you have spent within an industry, the more copious your knowledge of product applications, key classifications that distinguish different segments of customers, and so forth. In terms of ingenuity, it helps to envision yourself having conversations with articulate customers within the target population.

Simply write down what you would need to ask them to determine whether they were, for instance, satisfied or dissatisfied, and in what customer grouping they could best be placed.

Best Practices and Rules to Observe

The advice in this section is organized under three headings, with respect to the questionnaire as a whole, the phrasing of individual questions, and the selection and calibration of answer categories. The greater the likelihood that respondents will refuse to participate, or fail to complete the questionnaire, the more important these rules are. In that sense, many of these suggestions deal with how to motivate people to participate and how to keep them motivated through completion of the questionnaire. Most of the remainder concern ways to maximize the accuracy, meaningfulness, and actionability of the information obtained via the questionnaire.

THE QUESTIONNAIRE AS A WHOLE

1.Maximize the perceived rewards of responding, and minimize the perceived costs.

This general piece of advice is developed at length by Dillman (1999; see References and Suggested Readings in Chapter 7). The next few rules give some specific examples of how to do this. Reward maximization combined with cost minimization represents the fundamental formula for motivating respondents. As mentioned in Chapter 7, in the case of most questionnaires prepared for use in commercial market research, there really aren't very many rewards for the respondent, and the costs of participation, in terms of lost time and frustration, are immediate and very real. Hence, most questionnaires require an introduction that stresses the importance and value of the respondent's participation. It is more rewarding to participate in an important enterprise as opposed to a trivial one. If you can't write such an introduction with a straight face, or really don't believe what you've written, then I suggest you either ramp up the financial incentives for participating or consider whether the questionnaire is worth doing at all. How helpful will it be to analyze responses given by a few stubborn and opinionated respondents who persevered despite being bored to tears?

2. Shorter is better.

Every factor internal to your own corporate processes will tend to drive up questionnaire length. Everyone on the team has a pet topic; important bosses must be placated; the issues are complicated; the segmentation scheme is elaborate; there are numerous past studies with which you wish to be comparable; and so forth. To fight back, keep in mind that (a) survey costs are a power function of survey length—costs go up faster than the unit change in length, and beyond a certain length, costs skyrocket; (b) response rate and completion rate both drop rapidly as length increases—the lower these rates, the less reliable the information gained; and (c) the incidence of unthinking or essentially random responses increases rapidly once the survey comes to seem "long" in the respondent's eyes. In short, failure to trim back the questionnaire may ruin the entire study, so that little useful information is gained on even the most central and important issues.

As a rule of thumb, in print terms the questionnaire should be four pages or less. One page is a wonderful target but often not feasible. For phone questionnaires 15 minutes is a useful target, and five minutes, like the one-page questionnaire, is a wonderful target. It is certainly true that length restrictions can be relaxed when participation is to some degree compelled, either because of financial incentives or because the audience is to some degree captive. However, there remains a threshold beyond which the randomness of response increases rapidly.

3. Cluster the related content and seek a natural flow.

This is one of those small steps that can have a marked effect on the perceived cost and hassle factor of participation. If topics are addressed in essentially random order, and the questionnaire jumps back and forth between topics, the effect is wearisome.

4. Place demographic and other classification questions last.

However crucial to the analyses, these are the most boring questions imaginable from the standpoint of the typical respondent, and hence must be placed last.

5. Lead with questions that are clearly relevant, interesting, and nonthreatening.

If the initial questions stimulate thought (unlike a query about one's gender or age), and appear clearly important for a vendor to understand, then the perceived rewards of participation in the survey are enhanced. It comes to seem interesting and engaging, rather than tedious and off-putting.

6. Use plenty of white space and seek the most professional appearance possible consistent with time and budget.

White space makes the questionnaire seem easy to complete (i.e., minimizes the costs of participation). A professional appearance, with a layout that took some care and graphical elements not found in the typical memo, signals that the survey was important to the sponsor, which suggests to the respondents that they may likewise wish to respond thoughtfully and with some care. Anyone today can fire up a word processor, invoke a numbered and bulleted template, and obtain something that looks like a bona fide questionnaire as fast as one can type. But inevitably the message sent is, I didn't spend much time on this. What effect do you suppose that message has on the respondent?

Question Phrasing

1. Keep it simple.

Other things being equal, the shorter the question, the better. Plan on using simple language; targeting an eighth-grade reading level is about right. Now it is true that in technical industries, it may be necessary to use technical vocabulary, but that is no excuse for complicating the syntax. Even in the best of cases, the respondent is probably reading rapidly with less than full attention. You want to be understood despite these constraints.

Sometimes there is no choice but to depart from the ideal of simplicity. For instance, your questionnaire may need to include a branch (i.e., "If your answer is no, skip to Question X"). One branch will work if carefully handled, and maybe two. If you have more than two branches, nested branches, and so on, respondents will start dropping like flies. Remember, the easiest response when frustration or confusion occurs is to simply chuck the questionnaire. Hence, complexity is like length—it has to be fought every step of the way.

2. Be specific.

At the level of the individual question, this rule sometimes conflicts with the previous one. Consider, for instance, a simple approach to asking about income:

"How much do you make?"

It is hard to ask this question in fewer words! (Maybe, "What do you earn?") The problem is the vast range of possible answers, depending on how a given respondent interprets either question: Should I give my hourly rate? My annual salary? Should I include my bonus? What about dividends? We're a two-income household; does he want both? To eliminate such ambiguity, which would render the average answer meaningless (since in essence respondents were answering different questions), you are often forced into a lengthier phrasing that is less subject to ambiguity:

What was your total household income last year, including salaries, bonuses, dividends, and other income?

Although longer, the question is still clear and is more likely to produce usable information (allowing for the fact that no matter how you ask a question about income, some proportion of respondents will refuse to answer).

3. Ask mostly closed-ended questions.

A closed-ended question supplies specific answer categories that the respondent need only check off ("Which of the following kinds of documents have you created on your home PC?"). An open-ended question requires the respondent to generate and then to write in all the answers that pertain (i.e., "What documents have you created on your home PC?" followed by a series of blank lines). Open-ended questions, while ideal for qualitative research, are problematic in questionnaires, because they require so much more effort to respond, and are so subject to forgetting and to salience biases, making responses less comparable across respondents.

4. Minimize demands on memory.

If most respondents would have to consult some paper record to give a truly accurate answer, then the question needs to be rephrased. (Respondents won't consult a record, resulting in guesses of widely varying accuracy.) An example would be the question, "How many times did you eat out at a restaurant in the past six months?" Better would be to ask, "How many times did you eat dinner at a restaurant in the last month?" with answer categories of zero, once, twice, more often. This latter phrasing likely offers all the accuracy you can hope to obtain.

5. Match questions to how the market works.

Suppose you ask a question like, "How many brands of stuffing can you recall?" Many consumers, even avid homemakers, are likely to report "none." Does that mean that all the brand advertising in this category has been wasted? More likely, this is a product category where purchases are made by recognition rather than recall—when there is a need for stuffing, the shopper seeks out the aisle where this product is shelved, encounters the available packages, and only at that point retrieves from memory any relevant brand information. It is pointless in such a category to ask about recall; better to reproduce the packages or the brand names, complete with logo, and ask respondents to check any brands they recognize and any they have purchased during some time interval.

To give another example, in a technology context one may be interested in perceptions of the brand relative to its competitors, to the extent of wanting to ask in detail comparative questions about strengths and weaknesses of each brand. If the questionnaire goes to a manager, or to a member of a buying group that has recently had occasion to solicit bids from different vendors, then these questions may work just fine. If instead the questionnaire goes to individual users of the same vendors' products, in many cases these users will have experience of only one vendor, and may never have used any other vendor's product in this category. Nonetheless, many respondents will do their best to answer the questions about all the other vendors, despite near total ignorance. The result? Garbage.

6. Avoided loaded questions.

Loaded questions contain "angel" or "devil" words. For example:

Do you think the power of big union bosses needs to be curbed?

Or, for those of you of the alternative political persuasion:

Do you think fat cat executives should be allowed to ship American jobs overseas at will?

The best tone to strike is mild-mannered and matter-of-fact. Keep question phrasing as neutral as possible.

Answer Categories

1. Use the right number of answer categories, no more and no fewer than necessary.

For any given question, there is an optimum number of answer categories. Some factual questions, such as whether an event has occurred or something is present in the home, really are yes–no questions, and benefit from having exactly two answer categories. Other factual questions, such as education level, may require four or more answer categories (did not finish high school, high school grad, some college, college grad, master's, doctorate). When a question has four or more possible answers, it is almost always worth asking whether it would be better to collapse some of these categories. With respect to the education example, one can imagine many contexts in technology industries, or in the case of products targeted at affluent people, where a high portion of the respondents will have a college degree, and the only useful distinction is no college degree, college degree, graduate degree. In my experience beginning survey designers are excessively enamored with precision and with attempting to capture all possible categories of response, as in the education example. A helpful discipline is to look ahead to the ultimate analysis and make several mock-up tables involving the question. It is rare that very many 5×5 tables appear in commercial survey reports (or are interpretable when they do). Often the first thing that happens as analysis proceeds is that categories get collapsed in order to make important findings more salient; thus, the analyst, looking at the distribution of replies and finding many almost empty cells (i.e., less than high school education + income over $250,000 annually), and finding as well a breakpoint where results shift, quickly recodes the education variable as college degree: yes–no; and presents all further tables involving this variable in that two-column format, to highlight the fact that those without a college degree have very different responses. If this result can be anticipated, then you might as well reduce the number of answer categories on the questionnaire itself.

As a general rule, if categories are likely to be collapsed in the analysis, they might as well be collapsed in questionnaire design so as to simplify the respondent's task. Of course, this rule can be broken from time to time. Thus, one might distinguish college grads with and without graduate degrees, just in case having even more education accentuates the effect of interest, even as one is prepared to collapse these categories after the initial examination of the data. But if a designer makes this same choice every time, always proliferating categories "just in case," the questionnaire becomes longer and more unwieldy than necessary, with a lower response rate, and more respondent fatigue, adding more random noise to the answers. Hence, the thrust of this piece of advice is that fewer categories are better.

There is one other occasion where answer categories may be proliferated, and that is when this proliferation increases respondent comfort and ease. An important instance of this phenomenon occurs when we wish customers to react to various statements of opinion by agreeing or disagreeing. Technically speaking, there may be only three distinct responses to a statement such as "Microsoft software is too vulnerable to viruses"— agree, neither agree nor disagree, disagree.

However, when responding to a series of such items, respondents may start thinking, "I guess that's right, but I don't feel nearly as strongly as I did on the previous one, so maybe I should check 'neither'!" This obscures what we are trying to learn, which is this person's initial lean toward or away from the opinion proffered. Hence, when using agree–disagree items, it is standard practice to differentiate "strongly agree" from "agree" and "strongly disagree" from "disagree." This allows respondents to feel that their answers reflect distinctions in how strongly they feel about one opinion versus another, and increases their comfort that the survey is going to yield meaningful results, and hence is worth completing. However, pursuing this logic one more step, and using a seven-point scale for agree–disagree items, is generally a mistake. There isn't any consensus as to whether the responses should be labeled "strongly agree," "quite agree," and "sort of agree" (or by some other set of qualifiers), nor any stability in how these labels are interpreted by ordinary people. ("Quite" is a word that is quite a bit more common on campus than off.) The "fewer is better" rule applies again; stick to five categories (or sometimes four; see below) when using agree–disagree items.

2. Distinguish between bipolar and unipolar response types, and match answer categories to response type.

In my opinion, questionnaire designers have become way too fond of using the agree–disagree response format for every kind of question whatsoever (this vice is shared by academics as well as practitioners). However, good questionnaire design distinguishes between issues that have a natural pro or con element (for which the bipolar agree–disagree response is appropriate) and other issues where the underlying response continuum is unipolar, ranging from zero to a lot. Consider the difference between these question prompts:

"Baseball is a whole family sport."

"The Cubs will lose the World Series."

"I enjoy baseball."

Arguably, only the first statement is well suited to an agree–disagree format. It is a classic statement of an opinion that concerns an intangible predicate. The second statement is really a request for an assessment of probability, itself a unipolar judgment. One is asking for the respondent's subjective probability that the event will occur, and the logical response categories would be anchored by something such as "0% probability" and "100% probability." The third statement is really seeking to discover how well this description fits the respondent. The logical response scale is again unipolar, anchored by, "Does not describe me at all" and "Describes me very well." The point of these examples is that some questions admit of opposite responses, whereas in other cases responses vary only in terms of the degree to which they deviate from some zero point. The first may be appropriate for agree–disagree items; the second is not. Failure to attend to this difference undercuts the quality of the data collected.

3. Attend to the integration of the set of answer categories used for a question.

By integration I mean that the answer categories collectively have to be mutually exclusive, have to exhaust the possibilities for responding to the question, and must also not contain any superfluous or heterogeneous categories. The easiest way to convey this point is to illustrate typical violations. Consider the question "What is your age?"

Answer Set A	Answer Set B
<18	<18
19–25	18–25
25–34	26–35
35–44	36–45
45–54	46–55
>54	56–65
	Retired

With answer set A, there is no category for a person who is 18, and a person who is 25 has a choice of two categories. With answer set B, the very different category of retirement status is mixed in with categories that distinguish age. Errors of this sort are common in first drafts of questionnaires; it is one of the reasons why having other team members scrutinize a draft is so powerful.

4. Think carefully about whether to include a "don't know," "no opinion," or similar "not applicable" response category.

There are no simple hard-and-fast rules about when to include an "opt-out" response category. If I am asking respondents to rate their satisfaction with aspects of a service, not all of which may have been personally experienced by all respondents, I think it is good practice to include an opt-out response. Basically, if a respondent has never called tech support, they can't be either satisfied or dissatisfied with its responsiveness. If you omit the opt-out category, and include a neutral or mixed category (reasonable when measuring satisfaction), some proportion of the "neutral" responses will represent people with no experience of the service, who settled on the neutral category as the closest to "not applicable." The result is to muddy the data, especially when comparing service aspects that vary widely in the number of customers who have any experience of the aspect. There might be an aspect experienced by few, but very satisfying to those with experience, that comes across as a weak or problematic aspect, because of the number of people who wanted to check "not applicable" but settled on the middle category instead, resulting in a lower average score for that aspect.

Conversely, if I am seeking to discover whether customers lean one way or another with respect to some subjective evaluation where there is no factual right or wrong, and where anyone can have a viewpoint, without having had some specific kind of experience, I may choose to omit both the opt-out response and the neutral response, and use a four-point scale with two levels of agree and disagree. This is particularly true when seeking top-of-mind initial impressions about intangibles. For instance, when measuring brand perceptions, we might want to present a series of statements such as, "Apple is a fun brand," "Apple attracts people who think differently," and so forth. If given the neutral option, the more stolid respondents may well choose it, at different levels of frequency across different questions, saying to themselves something like "darned if I know." In fact, a great deal of brand knowledge is tacit, but sufficient for people to have a leaning one way or the other if forced. The intent of the question is precisely to tap into this tacit knowledge, and to do so uniformly across items and respondent temperaments. Hence, the utility of forcing respondents to lean one way or the other.

On the other hand, one can envision questions where many respondents genuinely have no opinion, because it is clearly an issue requiring some reflection, which they haven't had the opportunity for. Here an opt-out response makes sense because we may not be interested in the snap judgments of people who haven't really formed an opinion. Thus, a brokerage firm might present investors with a statement such as, "Do you favor having option prices quoted in minimum increments of one cent, as opposed to 5 cents and 10 cents, as is done currently?" An opt-out response will be gratefully accepted by many respondents in such an instance, and the proportion of investors who don't have an opinion on this score may be of interest in its own right.

I hope these three examples give some taste of the complexity involved in deciding whether to include an opt-out option. Most experienced practitioners are able to make a judgment in a specific case about whether an opt-out response is appropriate, but it is difficult to abstract a simple set of rules underlying these judgments.

5. In general, you should prefer ratings over rankings.

In ranking, say, the importance of each of a set of things, the respondent has to indicate which is most important, which is second most important, and so forth. If the number of items is five or greater, the task quickly grows demanding and wearisome. There is also little reason to believe that the fifth ranked item will reliably be placed above the sixth ranked item by this respondent; lower ranks tend to be "noisy," with a strong random component. It is far easier for a respondent to apply a rating scale where $0 =$ no importance and $6 =$ extremely important to a dozen statements than it would be to rank that same dozen from 1 to 12, or even to select the three most important items from the set of 12.

Ranking is one of those spuriously precise measurement approaches of which beginning questionnaire designers become enamored. It is not at all clear that most consumers, in most circumstances, natively use more than the first three ranks. Plus, from the standpoint of statistical analysis, ranks data are peculiarly gnarly. Hence, most of the time it is better to use a rating scale, and examine the ordering of average ratings across the sample to determine the rank order of individual items. The exceptions are when the number of things to be ranked is small ($= 4$), or when you have reason to believe that many items will be uniformly rated as "very important." Here a useful approach may be to present the list and ask respondents to place a "1" opposite the most important, "2" opposite the second most important, and "3" opposite the third most important. This forces respondents to prioritize among items, all of which are at least important. However, beyond listing the frequency with which an item received a "1," and the frequency with which items received any rank, analysis of such responses becomes difficult because of the statistical gnarliness, which is accentuated when the data consists not only of ranks, but of k out of n possible ranks.

Do's and Don'ts

Do take your time in the design phase. Questionnaires, like most significant design tasks, benefit from periods of digestion and time away from the task.

Don't let a desire for precision breed unnecessary complexity. Keep it simple.

Don't give in to a desire for comprehensive coverage. Keep it short.

Do ask yourself what is the single most important question in the questionnaire. Arrange things so that this question has the chance to receive the full attention of respondents.

Don't proliferate categorization variables needlessly. If there is no reason to suppose that gender influences the responses of these industrial buyers, and no intention of implementing a different marketing mix for men and women, don't include the question.

Do make mock-up tables showing which items will be used to break out responses on other items. If an item doesn't enter into any such breakout, is it necessary to include it?

Suggested Readings

Payne, Stanley L. 1951. *The Art of Asking Questions.* Princeton, NJ: Princeton University Press.

Classic, timeless book on effective and ineffective ways to word questions.

Sudman, Seymour, and Norman Bradburn. 1982. *Asking Questions: A Practical Guide to Questionnaire Design.* San Francisco: Jossey-Bass.

Converse, Jean M., and Stanley Presser. 1986. *Survey Questions: Handcrafting the Standardized Questionnaire.* Beverly Hills, CA: Sage.

These two books from recognized authorities focus on constructing questions, and introduce the empirical research on how people respond to various types of questions.

9

Choice Modeling via Conjoint Analysis

Conjoint analysis is the best-known example of a larger family of procedures that attempt to model the factors underlying consumer choice. Any procedure that attempts to analyze how different factors combine to influence the choice of one product over another can be considered a kind of choice modeling. The underlying assumption is that any product or service offering can be conceptualized as a bundle of attributes. Each of these attributes may be more or less important to any particular buyer, and each attribute may be possessed to a greater or lesser degree by any particular product offering. In general, attributes can be thought of as the components that make up the product's performance (e.g., how fast a computer is, how much memory it has, what software it can run, etc.), and also as points of difference that distinguish the offerings of various competitors (here more abstract attributes such as reliability, availability of support, and vendor reputation may come into play). All choice modeling procedures provide an estimate of the importance or the weight of each attribute in a buyer's purchase decision. Many procedures also allow one to simulate in-market results for a specific combination of attributes at a specified price.

Choice modeling is one of the newest market research procedures, and it is generally the least familiar to a managerial audience. Because it has been a focus of academic research and development (R&D), there are a large number of methods. In keeping with the approach of this book, we focus exclusively on a particular approach to choice modeling—conjoint analysis—and on one of the many possible implementations of it.

Designing a Conjoint Analysis Study

Let's suppose you are designing a new 17-inch LCD monitor intended to be purchased as an upgrade to a personal computer. Experience suggests that the following attributes may be influential:

1. Price

2. Brightness

3. Intensity of contrast

4. Latency of response in milliseconds

5. Analog or digital inputs

6. Width of the bezel surrounding the actual screen

7. Brightness control via physical button or software

Note that most of these features are nice to have, and the rest are matters of taste. It won't do you much good to conduct customer visits to see whether these features matter to buyers; you already know that they do matter. In fact, customer visits in combination with secondary research may have been the source of these attributes in the first place. What you don't know is precisely how important each attribute is. You also don't know which of these attributes is worth extra money, nor can you discern what the ideal combination of attribute levels and price point might be, or how consumers make trade-offs between attributes. A conjoint analysis study can potentially address all of these questions.

Given a set of design attributes to be studied, the next step is to decide how many levels of each attribute you will examine. The complexity of the study can quickly become unmanageable if too many levels of too many attributes are investigated. Even seven attributes, each with two levels, allows for 2^7, or 128 permutations of the LCD monitor design. Five attributes each having three levels would be even worse, with 243 permutations. In practice, consumers will not rate all possible permutations of the attribute. A technique known as fractional experimental design is used to reduce the number of permutations to a much more manageable number, perhaps as few as one or two dozen in these examples. Essentially, only the permutations that convey the maximal amount of information about how the attributes and levels contribute to choice are retained. (A statistician should be consulted if a fractional design is desired; the specific permutations that are best to use in a given case are not intuitively obvious if you are new to the technique). Alternatively, software has been designed that interactively determines the specific permutations that have to be presented to an individual respondent, based on the responses to the first few permutations presented. In either case, the effect is to make the consumer's task more feasible.

Regardless, it is still imperative that you simplify the design as much as possible. Although the number of permutations presented to the consumer can be kept to a low number, these permutations tacitly include the entire design. Reading 10 pieces of information, each of which may be present at three or four different levels across permutations, and then deciding just how much more one prefers the one permutation to the other, is many times more complex a judgment task than reading six pieces of information each of which has two possible states across permutations. This remains true, even if one is only rating a total of 15 permutations in each case. Excessive complexity breeds random responses on the part of participants, which, once submitted to statistical analysis, produce a very precise form of garbage.

Two considerations have to be balanced when setting levels of the attributes. On the one hand, you want to investigate all the relevant levels of an attribute. If response latencies of 12, 16, 20, or 25 milliseconds (ms) would have either very different implications for manufacturing costs or a significant impact on the usability or attractiveness of the monitor (i.e., the shorter the latency, the more effective the reproduction of moving images), then you have to include each of these levels in the design. On the other hand, if a latency of 25 ms is really not an option (perhaps because respected trade magazines are on record that anything slower than 20 ms is unacceptable, or because there is no difference in the manufacturing cost between 20 and 25 ms), then it need not be studied. From yet another angle, if the attribute levels are too far apart (i.e., you only study latencies of 12 and 20), then the conjoint analysis will not help you as much as it might have when it comes to selecting the optimal design (that is, you may find that 12 ms is strongly preferred, but you deny yourself the opportunity of discovering that the cheaper-to-manufacture latency of 16 ms would have been almost as strongly preferred). Then again, if you use attribute levels that are too close (i.e., you look at latencies of 12, 14, 16, and 18), consumers may apply a chunking rule, categorizing 12 and 14 as "real fast" and 16 and 18 as "kind of fast," proceeding from then on as if your conjoint design only had two levels of latency. In that event, you doubled the complexity of your design for no gain in understanding.

In practice, the number of attributes and levels actually studied is determined partly by your budget and partly by a sorting-out process wherein you determine what's really important to analyze and understand, and what can be taken for granted. Thus, you may decide not to study latency at all, reasoning that a latency of 12 ms is objectively superior, not much more expensive to manufacture than slower latencies, and in any case a strategic necessity given your business plan, which requires you to go head to head against competitor X, who has standardized on a latency of 12. If you reason thus, you might choose to simplify your design by dropping this attribute altogether.

Next, you create cards that correspond to all the permutations that you want to test. If the analysis will be administered by computer, then for "card" in this account substitute "screen." Again, a statistician or a specialist in conjoint analysis can help you devise a design that estimates all parameters of interest using the minimum number of permutations. Such a reduced design may include some absurd or unlikely permutations, if they serve the purpose of efficient statistical estimation. It may also include a few additional permutations, not required for statistical estimation, but useful for adding precision to an anticipated simulation (see below).

To continue our example, we now have perhaps 20 cards, each of which describes a possible video monitor design. Next, these cards will be administered to a good-sized sample (100+ people) drawn from the population of interest. Formulas similar to those discussed in Chapter 6 can be used to determine the necessary size. As always, sample characteristics are crucial. The people who participate in the conjoint study must represent the population for whom the LCD monitor is being designed. It is *their* choice process that we want to understand. No amount of powerful mathematics in the analysis stage can overcome the negative effects of a poor sample selection procedure.

Next, you determine what kind of rating or judgment procedure you want subjects to apply to the 20 monitor designs. Typically this will be a measure of preference; perhaps a 10-point scale where "10" indicates a very strong positive reaction to the design and a "1" equals a very strong negative reaction. Other measures, such as a rank ordering of the permutations, or even pairwise comparisons, are also possible. Note in passing that it may be important to vary the order of presentation of designs across subjects; items presented at the beginning and end of any judgment task are subject to well-known biases, and these need to be controlled.

A notable feature of conjoint analysis is that the response requested of subjects is very simple and straightforward: to assign a number indicating how much one likes some specific product design (compare the amount of cogitation it takes to complete the typical four-page survey). Although the conjoint task itself generally requires only a single judgment of each permutation, it is general practice to collect additional data on respondents. The information collected is of the sort used to profile customers (spending level, involvement with the product category, purchase plans) or segment markets (demographic and other descriptors). This information can be used in simulations and other follow-on analyses of the basic conjoint analysis, as described below.

Lastly, statistical analysis will be applied to determine utility weights for each attribute. In essence, the analysis considers the differences in expressed preferences and relates these back to variations in specific attributes. Was preference consistently higher whenever a design specified a faster monitor? If so, this attribute will have a high weight: it appears to be an important factor in choosing a monitor. Was there little or no difference in preference stemming from various levels of contrast? If so, the analysis will assign a low weight to this attribute. The analysis will also detect nonlinear preferences, that is, situations where preference is greatest for a middle level of some attribute. Perhaps a middle level of brightness is preferred to either a very bright or not very bright monitor. Part of the power of conjoint analysis is precisely that it allows you to estimate utility weights for each level of the attribute, and not just the attribute as a whole.

The analysis just described produces weights for each individual customer participating in the study. Because marketing strategies typically do not target individuals but either segments or entire markets, the final step in the conjoint study is to determine how the utility weights for individuals should be aggregated. If experience or inspection of the data suggest that preferences are relatively homogeneous, then one can simply lump all respondents together to determine average utility weights for each attribute. Alternatively, there may be reason to believe that there are two, three, or four quite different segments with distinct preferences. A statistical procedure known as cluster analysis can then be applied to the initial conjoint results. Cluster analysis separates respondents into groups based on the similarity of their utility weight profiles. Then, you can determine average utility weights for each attribute separately for each segment. This then indicates what the optimal product design would look like on a segment-by-segment basis. Additional data collected from respondents may assist in profiling and identifying these segments. Note that if you anticipate performing such a segmentation analysis, then a larger sample size, closer to 500, or even more, will be required.

As a result of the preceding steps, you will have learned which combination of attributes and levels is judged to be optimal by this sample of respondents. If price has been included, you can look at the optimal combinations of attributes and levels for each price point, and you can estimate how much a move from one level of an attribute to the next level of an attribute is worth to consumers in dollars and cents. Similarly, if price is given a low weight or importance by the analysis, then this suggests that demand is relatively inelastic in this category, within the price range investigated.

Optionally, analysis can be pushed to the next level, using what is sometimes labeled as simulation analysis. Simulations are particularly powerful if brand was among the attributes included in the conjoint analysis, and if one or more permutations can be taken to be a replica of a specific competitor's product. Essentially the simulation extrapolates from the results of the conjoint analysis to estimate market share for a hypothetical product relative to some competitive set (see Joachimsthaler and Green, 1993, for a detailed example). Given an estimate of market share, we can estimate revenues; given an estimate of revenues and knowledge of probable costs, we can apply a hurdle rate to determine if even the "best" new product design is worth doing, and we can make a forecast of income to be expected from the product once introduced. In short, the use of simulation techniques allows conjoint analyses, like experimentation, to answer two questions: not only, Which one is best? but also, How much will we achieve (with the best)?

Strengths and Weaknesses

The great strength of conjoint analysis is the amount of complexity that these procedures can incorporate. This is most clearly seen if one contrasts conjoint analysis with an attempt to get at the same kind of information through a series of customer visits. Human beings simply aren't that good at thoroughly explicating how they weight various factors in coming to a decision, or what sort of combination rule they apply for integrating information. Nor are human beings (the data analysts in this case) all that good at integrating a mass of interview data so as to precisely delineate different choice models across several segments within a market. Customer visits *would* be quite effective at identifying attributes that matter, and explaining why they matter, and even at explaining why a customer might trade off in favor of one attribute rather than another. Customer visits could also help the data analyst glimpse the possibility that several different segments exist and what some key points of difference might be. But customer visits would be unlikely ever to provide the analytic precision that conjoint analysis so readily offers.

Another way to explain this key strength is that conjoint analysis goes beyond the customer's self-report. Rather, the consumer is given the opportunity to act within a carefully constructed situation, and then powerful mathematical techniques are applied to the task of understanding those actions by decomposing them into preferences for specific levels of the attributes considered.

Conjoint analysis represents the acme of the application of modern statistical analysis to the solution of enduring business and marketing questions, such as how to design winning products and how to improve existing product offerings. It provides one of the clearest instances of the practical payoff of academically driven R&D within the marketing profession. Thirty years ago, it was practically impossible to do what anyone with a personal computer and a good statistical background can readily do today. Although conjoint analysis is hardly a panacea, it is difficult to imagine a substantial product design effort (absent the caveats and limiting conditions cited below) that would not benefit from some type of choice modeling initiative. A particular advantage of conjoint analysis procedures is the ability to deal with and sort through a large number of product design alternatives. This strength is most evident in contrast to the controlled experiments described in the next chapter.

Conjoint analysis also offers an interesting mix of confirmatory and exploratory opportunities. Although predominately a confirmatory technique in the sense that findings are constrained by your initial choices concerning what attributes to study, within those constraints it is possible to explore via simulation the probable outcome of making any number of changes in product design and positioning. A study done at the level of a product platform (i.e., the technological base from which several generations of specific product models will issue) may provide useful simulation opportunities for some time.

The most important weaknesses of conjoint analysis can be thought of as limits or constraints. Two are particularly crucial: the sample of customers used and the set of attributes examined. Just as a biased sample in a survey renders suspect or useless any number of precise percentage breakdowns, so also a biased sample in a conjoint analysis study could lead to seriously misleading results, as you precisely describe the choice process of an idiosyncratic (and perhaps small) subsegment of the overall market. An even more fundamental limitation concerns the set of attributes chosen for study. Here the garbage in–garbage out rule applies: if crucial attributes are omitted, or if the wrong levels are set, or if the attributes are poorly stated or are misinterpreted by customers, then the results may be of little value.

Less crucial, but important to remember, is the fact that conjoint analysis can take a long time and cost a large amount of money. (Although, like surveys, cost and time frame are actually highly variable, a straightforward conjoint analysis on a single segment might not cost any more than a good focus group study.)

Lastly, conjoint analysis can be difficult to implement for products purchased through a group decision process. And it is necessary to assume that buyers process the information presented to them in the conjoint analysis exercise in the same way that they process that information in actual buying decisions. This assumption may not hold for buyers who have little experience with a product category, for products where market conditions are in flux or rapidly changing, or in the case of extremely new products whose implications may be difficult to grasp. For instance, just imagine yourself participating in a conjoint analysis aimed at designing a smart phone (cell phone plus personal organizer) in 1989.

Another limit particularly relevant to business-to-business and technology products concerns complexity. To be feasible, most conjoint studies have to be limited to half a dozen attributes with two or three levels. Now imagine an enterprise-planning software package such as those marketed by SAP, IBM, and Oracle. Such a product may have a hundred or more "attributes" all of which can be varied as the design team considers how version $N + 1$ might be improved over the current version. Conjoint analysis can assist in such a design task only to the extent that we can boil down competing design alternatives to a small number of key design choices ("attributes") that (1) can be readily apprehended by customers (an attribute is probably not suitable for conjoint analysis if it requires a multipage explanation) and (2) can be formulated as levels—at least, as the presence or absence of the attribute.

Do's and Don'ts

Don't try to put together the attributes for use in a choice modeling study by huddling around a white board with your colleagues. Do go out into the field and use customer visits, focus groups, and other exploratory techniques to identify these attributes and ascertain the words customers use to represent them.

Don't assume that any convenience sample of potential customers will do. Strive to get the best possible sample in terms of representing the population to which you want to appeal.

Don't be hasty in assuming that choice criteria and preference structures are basically the same for most buyers in the market. Do allow for the possibility of significant differences across segments.

References and Suggested Readings

Dolan, Robert J. 1999. *Analyzing Consumer Preferences.* HBS #9-599-112. Cambridge, MA: HBS Publishing.

An excellent and accessible introduction to how conjoint analysis can be interpreted to guide marketing decisions.

Green, Paul E., and Abba M. Krieger. 1991. Segmenting markets with conjoint analysis. *Journal of Marketing* 55 (October): 20–31.

Recommendations illustrated with examples for how to segment markets using conjoint analysis.

Green, Paul E., and V. Srinivasan. 1990. Conjoint analysis in marketing: New developments with implications for research and practice. *Journal of Marketing* 54 (October): 3–19.

Overview of the variety of approaches to conjoint analysis now available. The *Journal of Marketing Research* can be consulted for the latest developments in methodologies.

Joachimsthaler, Erich, and Paul Green. 1993. *New Ways to Answer Old Questions.* HBS #594-003. Cambridge, MA: HBS Publishing.

Gives an extended example of how simulation analyses can be applied to the results of a conjoint study.

See also the review of conjoint software packages by F. J. Carmone and C. M. Schaffer, 1995, in *Journal of Marketing Research* 32: 113–120, for an introduction to some of the packages available. Sawtooth software and SPSS are two noted suppliers of conjoint software, and their Web sites can be consulted for details of current offerings.

10

Experimentation

Experiments can be conducted in the field or in some kind of laboratory, that is, an artificial situation constructed by the researcher. The essence of any experiment is the attempt to arrange conditions in such a way that one can infer causality from the results. In practice this means creating conditions or treatments that differ in one precise respect, and then measuring some outcome of interest across the different conditions or treatments. Differences in that outcome (how many people buy, how many people prefer) can then be attributed unambiguously to the difference between the treatments. In a word, the experiment shows that the treatment difference *caused* the observed outcomes to differ. More properly, we should say that the treatment difference *probably* caused the outcomes to differ (the role of probability in hypothesis testing will be discussed in Chapter 11).

Experimentation should be considered whenever you want to compare a small number of alternatives in order to select the best. Three common examples would be selecting the best advertisement from among a pool of several, selecting the optimal price point, and selecting the best from among several product designs (the latter case is often referred to as a "concept test"). To conduct an experiment in any of these cases you would arrange for equivalent groups of customers to be exposed to the ads, prices, or product designs being tested. The ideal way to do this would be by randomly assigning people to the various conditions. When random assignment is not possible some kind of matching strategy can be employed. For instance, two sets of cities can provide the test sites, with the cities making up each set selected to be as similar as possible in terms of size of population, age and ethnicity of residents, per capita income, and so on. It has to be emphasized that an experiment is only as good as its degree of control; if the two groups being compared are not really equivalent, or if the treatments differ in several respects, some of them unintended (perhaps due to problems of execution or implementation), then it will no longer be possible to say whether the key treatment difference caused the difference in outcomes, or whether one of those other miscellaneous differences was in fact the cause. *Internal validity* refers to this kind of issue—our reasons for believing that the specified difference in treatments really did cause the difference in outcomes.

Because experiments are among the less familiar forms of market research, and because many of the details of implementing an experiment are carried out by specialists, it seems more useful to give extended examples rather than walking you through the procedural details, as has been done in other chapters. The examples address three typical applications for experimentation selecting among advertisements, price points, or product designs. First, however, it may be useful to compare conjoint analysis to experimentation, because many of the questions that get addressed through experimentation could potentially be addressed via conjoint analysis instead.

Experimentation Versus Conjoint Analysis

A substantial number of research questions, especially in the area of product design, can be addressed by either the experimentation procedures discussed in this chapter or the conjoint methodology discussed in Chapter 9. This is because the typical conjoint study represents a special kind of experimental design. There are two rules of thumb that may help you to decide whether to use mainstream methods of experimentation or a conjoint methodology. The first rule is that experimentation only makes sense if the number of distinct alternatives to be tested is very small. Six is probably a practical maximum, and the bulk of commercially conducted experiments probably examine two or three alternatives. As the number of alternatives increases beyond three, these probably represent permutations and combinations of some set of elements, and the conjoint methodology is a much more powerful means of evaluating all possible permutations of a set of elements.

The second rule that may incline you to choose *field* experiments is that conjoint analysis as currently implemented is always a laboratory technique. Consumers respond to abstract representations of products by giving ratings or other kinds of judgment that do not involve the expenditure of limited funds or time. By contrast, in many field experiments, respondents engage in behaviors in the market, or in some approximation to real consumption behavior. Those behaviors are closer to what the mass of consumers have to do when we take the results of the experiment to the market, and thus our confidence may be higher that marketplace results will replicate the experimental results. *External validity* refers to this kind of issue: to what extent will the outcomes in the marketplace mirror the outcomes in the experiment?

Example 1: Crafting Direct Mail Appeals

This is one type of experiment that virtually any business that uses direct mail appeals, however large or small, can conduct. (The logic of this example applies equally well to E-mail marketing, banner ads, and any other form of direct marketing.) All you need is a supply of potential customers that numbers in the hundreds or more. First, recognize that any direct mail appeal is made up of several components, for each of which you can imagine various alternatives: what you say on the outside of the envelope, what kind of headline opens the letter, details of the discount or other incentive, and so forth. Let's imagine that you are torn between using one of two headlines in your next direct mail effort:

1. "For a limited time you can steal this CCD chip."
2. "Now get the CCD chip rated #1 in reliability."

These represent, respectively, a low-price versus a high-quality lead-in. The remainder of each version of the letter will be identical. Let's further assume that the purpose of the campaign is to promote an inventory clearance sale prior to a model changeover.

To conduct an experiment to determine which of these appeals is going to produce a greater customer response, you might do the following. First, select two samples of, say, 150 or more customers from the mailing lists you intend to use, using formulas similar to those discussed in the sampling chapter. A statistician can help you compute the exact sample size you need (larger samples allow you to detect even small differences in the relative effectiveness of the two appeals, but larger samples also cost more). Next, you would use a probability sampling technique to draw names for the two samples; for instance, selecting every tenth name from the mailing list you intend to use for the campaign, with the first name selected assigned to treatment 1, the second to treatment 2, the third to treatment 1, and so forth. Note how this procedure is more likely to produce equivalent groups than, say, assigning everyone whose last name begins with A through L to treatment 1 and everyone whose last name begins with M through Z to treatment 2. It's easy to see how differences in the ethnic backgrounds of the A to L and M to Z groups might interfere with the comparison of treatments by introducing extraneous differences that have nothing to do with the effectiveness or lack thereof of the two headlines under study.

Next, create and print two alternative versions of the mailing you intend to send out. Make sure that everything about the two mailings is identical except for the different lead-in: same envelope, mailed the same day from the same post office, and so forth. Be sure to provide a code so that you can determine the treatment group to which each responding customer had been assigned. This might be a different extension number if response is by telephone, a code number if response is by postcard, and so forth. Most important, be sure that staff who will process these replies understand that an experiment is under way and that these codes must be carefully tracked.

After some reasonable interval, tally the responses to the two versions. Perhaps 12 of 150 customers responded to the high-quality appeal, whereas only 5 of 150 customers responded to the low-price appeal. A statistical test can then determine whether this difference, given the sample size, is big enough to be trustworthy (see Chapter 11). Next, implement the strongest treatment on a large scale for the campaign itself, secure in the knowledge that you are promoting your sale using the most effective headline *from among those considered.*

Commentary

The example just given represents a field experiment: real customers, acting in the course of normal business and unaware that they were part of an experiment, had the opportunity to give or withhold a real response: to buy or not to buy. Note the role of statistical analysis in determining sample size and in assessing whether differences in response were large enough to be meaningful. Note finally the assumption that the world does not change between the time when the experiment was conducted and the time when the actual direct mail campaign is implemented. This assumption is necessary if we are to infer that the treatment that worked best in the experiment will also be the treatment that works best in the campaign. If, in the meantime, a key competitor has made some noteworthy announcement, then the world has changed and your experiment may or may not be predictive of the world today.

In our example the experiment, assuming it was successfully conducted, that is, all extraneous differences were controlled for, establishes that the "Rated #1 in reliability" headline was more effective than the "Steal this chip" headline. Does the experiment then show that quality appeals are generally more effective than low-price appeals in this market? No, the experiment only establishes that *this* particular headline did better than this *other* particular headline. Only if we did many such experiments, using many varieties of "low price" and "quality" headlines, and getting similar results each time, might we tentatively infer that low-price appeals in general are less effective in this market. This one experiment alone cannot establish that generality. You should also recognize that the experiment in no way establishes that the "Rated #1 in reliability" headline is the *best possible* headline to use; it only shows that this headline is better than the one it was tested against. The point here is that experimentation, as a confirmatory technique, logically comes late in the decision process, and should be preceded by an earlier more generative stage where possible direct mail appeals are identified and explored, so that the appeals finally submitted to an experimental test are known to be credible and viable. Otherwise, you may be expending a great deal of effort merely to identify the lesser of two evils.

The other advantage offered by many experiments, especially field experiments, is that in addition to answering the question, Which one is best?, they also answer the question, How much will we achieve (with the best)? In the direct mail example, the high-quality appeal was responded to by 12 out of 150, giving a projected response rate of 8%.

This number, which will have a confidence interval around it, can be taken as a predictor of what the response rate in the market will be. If corporate planning has a hurdle rate of 10%, for proposed direct mail campaigns, then the direct mail experiment has both selected the best headline and also indicated that it is probably not worth doing a campaign with even the best of the headlines under consideration.

Much more elaborate field experiments than the direct mail example can be conducted with magazine and even television advertisements. All that is necessary is the delivery of different advertising treatments to equivalent groups and a means of measuring outcomes. Thus, split cable and "single source" data have become available in the past decade. In split cable a cable TV system in a geographically isolated market has been wired so that half the viewers can receive one advertisement while a different advertisement is shown to the other half. Single source data adds to this a panel of several thousand consumers in that market. These people bring a special card when they go shopping for groceries. It is handed to the cashier so that the optical scanner at the checkout records under their name every product that they buy. Because we know which consumers received which version of the advertisement, we can determine empirically which version of the ad was more successful at stimulating purchase. See Lodish et al., (1995) for more on split cable experiments. For an example of a magazine advertising experiment in a business-to-business context, see Maples and Wolfsberg (1987).

One way to grasp the power of experimentation is to consider what alternative kinds of market research might have been conducted in this case. For instance, suppose we had done a few focus groups. Perhaps we had a larger agenda of understanding the buying process for CCD chips, and decided to include a discussion of alternative advertising appeals, with a focus on the two headlines being debated. Certainly, at some point in each focus group discussion we could take a vote between the two headlines. However, from the earlier discussion in the sampling chapter, it should be apparent that a focus group is a decisively inferior approach to selecting the best appeal among two or three alternatives. The sample is too small to give any precision, and the discussion process is too variable between groups and too prone to biases (what do you suppose happens to the vote if the first person to speak up in the group says, "Oh, come on, that 'steal this product' kind of appeal is so lame!").

The focus groups may give some insight into the kinds of reaction people will have to each appeal, but that is not our concern at this point. This kind of focus group discussion might have been useful earlier, if our goal were to generate a variety of possible appeals, but at this point, we simply want to learn which of the two appeals is best.

We could alternatively have tried to examine the attractiveness of these appeals using some kind of survey. Presumably, in one section of the survey, we would list these two headlines and ask respondents to rate each one. Perhaps we would anchor the rating scale with phrases such as "high probability I would respond to this offer" and "zero probability I would respond." The problem with this approach is different from that in the case of focus groups—after all, the survey may obtain a sample that is just as good as the sample used in the experiment. The difficulty here lies with interpreting customer ratings obtained via a survey as a prediction of whether the mass of customers would buy or not buy in response to an in-the-market implementation of these offers. The problem is again one of external validity: First, the headline is not given in the context of the total offer, as it occurs within an artificial context (completing a survey rather than going through one's mail). Second, there is no reason to believe that respondents have any good insight into the factors that determine whether or not they respond to specific mail offers. (You say you never respond to junk mail? Huh, me neither! Hmmm, I wonder why there is so much of it out there . . .)

Remember, surveys are a tool for description. When you want prediction—which offer will work best—you seek out an experiment. If it is a field experiment, then the behavior of the sample in the experiment is virtually identical, except for time of occurrence, to the behavior you desire to predict among the mass of customers in the marketplace. Although prediction remains irreducibly fallible, the odds of predictive success are much higher in the case of a field experiment than if a survey or focus group were to be used for purposes of predicting some specific subsequent behavior.

Example 2: Selecting the Optimal Price

Pricing is a topic that is virtually impossible to research in a customer visit or other interview. If asked, "How much would you be willing to pay for this?," you should expect the rational customer to lie and give a low-ball answer! Similarly, the absurdity of asking a customer, "Would you prefer to pay $5,000 or $6,000 for this system?" should be readily apparent. Experimentation offers one solution to this dilemma; conjoint analysis offers another, as described earlier.

The key to conducting a price experiment is to create different treatment conditions whose *only* difference is a difference in price. Marketers of consumer packaged goods are often able to conduct field experiments to achieve this goal. Thus, a new snack product might be introduced in three sets of two cities, and only in those cities. The three sets are selected to be as equivalent as possible, and the product is introduced at three different prices, say, $2.59, $2.89, and $3.19. All other aspects of the marketing effort (advertisements, coupons, personal sales) are held constant across the three conditions, and sales are then tracked over time. While we would, of course, expect more snack food to be sold at the $2.59 price, the issue is *how much more*. If our cost of goods is $1.99, so that we earn a gross profit of 60 cents per package at the $2.59 price, then the low-price $2.59 package must sell at twice the level of the high-price $3.19 package (where we earn $1.20 per package) in order to yield the same total amount of profit. If the experiment shows that the $2.59 package has sales volume only 50% higher than the $3.19 package, then we may be better off with the higher price. Note how in this example the precision of estimate supplied by experimentation is part of its attraction.

Business-to-business and technology marketers often are not able to conduct a field experiment as just described. Their market may be national or global, or product introductions may be so closely followed by a trade press that regional isolation cannot be obtained. Moreover, because products may be very expensive, and hence dependent on personal selling, it may not be possible to set up equivalent treatment conditions. (Who would believe that the 10 salespeople given the product to sell at $59,000 are going to behave in a manner essentially equivalent to the 10 given it to sell at $69,000 and the 10 given it to sell at $79,000?) Plus, product life cycles may be so compressed that an in-the-market test is simply not feasible. As a result, laboratory experiments, in which the situation is to some extent artificial, have to be constructed in order to run price experiments in the typical business-to-business or technology situation. Here is an example of how you might proceed.

First, write an experimental booklet in which each page gives a brief description of a competitive product. The booklet as a whole should describe all the products that might be considered as alternatives to your product, with one page in the booklet describing your own product. The descriptions should indicate key features, *including price,* in a neutral, factual way. The goal is to provide the kind of information that a real customer making a real purchase decision would gather and use.

Next, select a response measure. For instance, respondents might indicate their degree of buying interest for each alternative, or how they would allocate a fixed sum of money toward purchases among these products. Various measures can be used in this connection; the important thing is that the measure provide some analogue of a real buying decision. This is why you have to provide a good description of each product: to make responses on the buying interest measure as meaningful as possible.

Now you create different versions of the booklet by varying the price. In one example, a manufacturer of handheld test meters wished to investigate possible prices of $89, $109, and $139, requiring three different versions of the booklet. Next, recruit a sample of potential customers to participate in the experiment. This sample must be some kind of probability sample drawn from the population of potential customers. Otherwise the responses are useless for determining the best price. Moreover, members of the sample must be randomly assigned to the treatment groups. If administration is to be by mail, it also makes sense to see whether the types of individuals who respond to the three treatments remain equivalent. If one type of buyer has tended to drop out of one treatment condition, for whatever reason, confidence in the results is correspondingly reduced. Finally, administer the experimental booklet. This could be done by mail or on the Web. It could also be done in person at a central site(s).

In this price example, to analyze the results you would examine differences in the projected market share for the product at each price (i.e., the percentage of respondents who indicate an interest or who allocate dollars to the product, relative to response to the competitive offerings). To understand the results, extrapolate from the projected market shares for the product at each price point to what unit volume would be at that level of market share. For example, the $89 price might yield a projected market share of 14%, corresponding to a unit volume of 76,000 handheld test meters. Next, construct an income statement for each price point. This will indicate the most profitable price. Thus, the $109 price may yield a market share of only 12%, but this smaller share, combined with the higher margin per meter, yields a larger total profit.

What we are doing by means of this experiment is investigating the *price elasticity* of demand, that is, how changes in price affect demand for the product. Of course, demand will probably be lower at the $109 price than the $89 price; the question is, Exactly how much lower? You might find that essentially no one is interested in the product at the highest price tested. In other words, demand is very elastic, so that interest drops off rapidly as the price goes up a little. The experiment in that case has averted disaster. Or (as actually happened in the case of the handheld test meter example) you might find that projected market share was almost as great at the $139 price as at the $89 price, with much higher total profit (which is only to say that demand proved to be quite inelastic). In this case the experiment would save you from leaving a great deal of money on the table through overly timid pricing.

Commentary

Whereas a direct mail experiment can be conducted by almost any businessperson with a little help from a statistician, you can readily understand why, in a semi-laboratory experiment such as just described, you might want to retain an outside specialist. Finding and recruiting the sample, and ensuring as high a return rate as possible, are nontrivial skills. Selecting the best response measure takes some expertise as well. In fact, a firm with a long track record can probably provide the additional service of comparing your test results with norms accumulated over years of experience.

Note that your level of confidence in extrapolating the results of a laboratory experiment will almost always be lower than in the case of a field experiment. In the direct mail example, the experiment provided an exact replica of the intended campaign, except that it occurred at a different point in time with a subset of the market. A much larger gulf has to be crossed in the case of inferences from a laboratory experiment. You have to assume that (1) the people in the sample do represent the population of potential customers; (2) their situation of receiving a booklet and perusing it does capture the essentials of what goes on during an actual purchase; and (3) the response given in the booklet does represent what they would actually do in the marketplace if confronted with these products at these prices. By contrast, in the direct mail case the sample can easily be made representative, as it is drawn from the same list; the experimental stimulus is identical with the real ad to be used; and the experimental response is identical to the actual response—purchase. Nonetheless, when field experiments are not possible, laboratory experiments may still be far superior to relying on your gut feeling—particularly when your gut feeling does not agree with the gut feeling of a respected and influential colleague.

Finally, the difficulty and expense of conducting a laboratory-style price experiment has pushed firms toward the use of conjoint analysis when attempting to estimate demand at various price points. This application of conjoint analysis makes use of simulations, as discussed in Chapter 9.

Example 3: Concept Testing—Selecting a Product Design

Suppose that you have two or three product concepts that have emerged from a lengthy development process. Each version emphasizes some kinds of functionality over others, or delivers better performance in some applications than in others. Each version has its proponents or partisans among development staff, and each version can be character-ized as responsive to customer input obtained through earlier qualita-tive and exploratory research. In such a situation you would again have two related questions: first, which one is best, and second, what is the sales potential of that best alternative (a forecasting question). The sec-ond question is important because you might not want to introduce even the best of the three alternatives unless you were confident of achieving a certain sales level or a certain degree of penetration into a specific competitor's market share.

Generally speaking, the same approach described under the pricing sample can be used to select among these product designs. If you can introduce an actual working product into selected marketplaces, as consumer goods manufacturers can, then this would be described as a *market test*. If you must make do with a verbal description of a product, then this would be described as a *concept test*. Whereas in the pricing example you would hold your product description constant and vary the price across conditions, in this product development example you would vary your product description across three conditions, while you would *probably* hold price constant. Of course, if your intent was to charge a higher price for one of the product designs to reflect its presumed delivery of greater functionality, then the price would vary along with the description of functionality.

Note, however, that the experimental results can only address the differences between the complete product descriptions as presented; if these descriptions differ in more than one respect, the experiment in no way tells you *which* respect caused the outcomes observed. Thus, suppose that you find that the high-functionality, high-price product design yields exactly the same level of customer preference as the medium-functionality, medium-price design. At least two explanations, which unfortunately have very different managerial implications, would then be viable: (1) the extra functionality had no perceived value, and the price difference was too small to have an effect on preference; or (2) the extra functionality did stimulate greater preference, which was exactly balanced by the preference-retarding effect of the higher price. You would kick yourself for not having included a high-functionality, medium-price alternative, which would have allowed you to disentangle these effects. Of course, if it would be desirable to vary price and functionality across multiple levels, you might be better off pursuing a conjoint analysis rather than a concept test.

It has to be emphasized that when an experiment is planned, the cleanest and most certain inferences can be drawn when the product designs being tested differ in exactly one respect, such as the presence or absence of a specific feature or functionality. If both product design and price are an issue, then it may be best to run two successive experiments, one to select a design and a second to determine price, or to run a more complex experiment in which both product design and price are systematically varied—that is, an experiment with six conditions composed of three product designs each at two price levels. At this point, however, many practitioners would again be inclined to design a conjoint study instead of an experiment. In terms of procedure, the product design experiment can be conducted by mail, as in the price example, or, at the extreme, at a central site using actual working prototypes and examples of competitor products.

Commentary

There is an important problem with concept testing of the sort just described if we examine the situation faced by most business-to-business (BTB) and technology firms. Market tests, if they can be conducted, are not subject to the following concern, but we agreed earlier that in many cases BTB and technology firms cannot conduct market tests of the sort routinely found among consumer packaged goods firms. The problem with concept tests, in BTB and technology contexts, lies with the second of the two questions that experiments can address (i.e., Which is best? versus How much will we achieve with the best?). We may assume that BTB concept tests are neither more nor less capable than consumer concept tests at differentiating the most preferred concept among the set tested. External validity issues are certainly present, but they are the same as when consumers in a test kitchen read descriptions of three different kinds of yogurt and indicate which is preferred. The problem comes when we attempt to generate a sales forecast from the measure of preference used in the concept test. That is, generalizing the *absolute* level of preference is a different matter than generalizing the *rank order* of preferences for some set of concepts.

Consumer packaged goods firms have a solution to this problem. Over the several decades that modern concept testing procedures have been in place, so many tests have been performed that leading research firms have succeeded in compiling databases that link concept test results to subsequent marketplace results. The data have become sufficiently rich that the concept test vendors have developed norms, on a product-by-product basis, for translating responses on the rating scale in the laboratory into market share and revenue figures in the market. The point is that the rating scale results in raw form cannot be extrapolated in any straightforward way into marketplace numbers. Thus, consumers' response to each tested concept may be summed up in a rating scale anchored by "Definitely would buy"/"Definitely would not buy." For the winning concept, 62% of consumers might have checked "Definitely would buy." Does this mean that the product will achieve 62% trial when introduced? Nope. Only when that 62% number is arrayed against past concept tests involving yogurt are we able to determine that historically this is actually a below-average preference rating for yogurt concepts (it might have been quite good for potato chips), that will likely only translate into a real trial rate of 29%, given the database findings.

There is no straightforward algorithm for translating rating scale responses, for a never-before-tested category, into a sales forecast. As most BTB firms are new to such market research arcana as concept tests, this means that the necessary norms probably do not exist, making concept test results less useful than for consumer goods manufacturers. (By definition, an innovative technology product cannot have accumulated many concept tests, so the point applies in spades to technology firms.) Thus, BTB and technology firms are encouraged to explore the possible uses of concept tests, but cautioned to use them mostly for differentiating better from worse concepts. Absent historical norms, one of the most attractive features of experiments, which involves projecting the absolute level of preference for purposes of constructing a market forecast, is simply not feasible.

Discussion

With the product design example in hand, it may be instructive to examine once again the merits of a controlled experiment as compared to choice modeling via conjoint analysis. The most important limitation of controlled experiments is that you are restricted to testing a very small number of alternatives. You also are limited to an overall thumbs-up or thumbs-down on the alternative as described. In conjoint studies you can examine a large number of permutations and combinations. Conjoint analysis is also more analytic: it estimates the contribution of each product component to overall preference, rather than simply rendering an overall judgment as to which concept scored best. Conversely, an advantage of controlled experiments is the somewhat greater realism of seeing product descriptions embedded in a context of descriptions of actual competitive products. Similarly, product descriptions can often be lengthier and more representative of the literature buyers will actually encounter, unlike conjoint analysis, where sparse descriptions are preferred in order to foreground the differences in level and type of product attribute that differentiate the design permutations under study.

Strengths and Weaknesses

Experimentation has one crucial advantage that is so simple and straightforward that it can easily be overlooked or underplayed: experiments yield causal knowledge. Experiments predict what will happen if you do X or choose Y. Although strictly speaking even experiments do not offer the kind of proof available in mathematics, experiments provide perhaps the most compelling kind of evidence available from any kind of market research, with field experiments being particularly strong on this count. In short, experiments represent a straightforward application of the scientific method to marketing decisions.

Experimentation has two subsidiary strengths. First, the structure of an experiment corresponds to one of the knottiest problems faced in business decision making: selecting the best from among several attractive alternatives. This is the kind of decision that, in the absence of experimental evidence, is particularly prone to politicking, to agonizing uncertainty, or to a despairing flip of the coin. In their place, experiments offer empirical evidence for distinguishing among good, better, and best. Second, experiments afford the opportunity to forecast sales, profit, and market share (again, this is most true of field experiments.) The direct mail experiment described earlier provides a forecast or prediction of what the return rate, and hence the profitability, will be for the campaign itself. The pricing experiment similarly provides a prediction of what kind of market share and competitive penetration one can achieve at a specific price point, while the product design experiment provides the same kind of forecast for a particular configuration of functionality. These forecasts can be used to construct pro forma income statements for the advertising, pricing, or product decision, and these in turn can be compared with corporate standards or expectations to make a go–no-go decision (i.e., even the best of the product designs tested may produce too little revenue or profit to be worthwhile). Other forecasting methods (e.g., extrapolation from historical data or expert opinion) are much more inferential and subject to greater uncertainty.

It must be emphasized that the predictive advantage of experiments is probably greatest in the case of field experiments. Laboratory experiments, when the goal is to predict the absolute level of response in the marketplace, raise many issues of external validity. By contrast, in academic contexts where theory testing is of primary interest, laboratory experiments may be preferred because of considerations of internal validity.

Experimentation is not without weaknesses. These mostly take the form of limits or boundary cases beyond which experimentation simply may not be feasible. For example, suppose there are only 89 "buyers" worldwide for your product category. In this case, you probably cannot construct two experimental groups large enough to provide statistically valid inferences, and sufficiently isolated to be free of reactivity (reactivity occurs when buyers in separate groups discover that an experiment is going on and compare notes). In general, experiments work best when there is a (large) population from which to sample respondents. A second limit concerns products bought by committees or groups. It obviously does you little good if an experiment haphazardly samples fragments of these buying groups. You must either pick one kind of participant, and confine the experiment to that kind, with consequent limits on your understanding, or find a way to get groups to participate in the experiment, which dramatically increases the costs and complexity.

More generally, experiments only decide between options that you input. Experiments do not generate fresh options and they do not indicate the optimal possible alternative—they only select the best alternative from among those specified. This is not a problem when experiments are used correctly as the culmination of a program of research, but it can present difficulties if you rush prematurely into an experiment without adequate preparation. A related problem is that one can only select among a quite small number of alternatives. Conjoint analysis is a better route to go if you want to examine a large number of possibilities. Lastly, experiments can take a long time to conduct and can potentially tip off competitors, especially when conducted in the field.

Do's and Don'ts

Don't be overhasty in arranging to do an experiment. You really have to know quite a lot about customers and the market before an experiment can be valuable. If conducted prematurely, you risk getting wonderfully precise answers to the wrong question.

Don't let fear of costs prevent you from doing an experiment where appropriate. A laboratory experiment such as the price and product design examples described earlier may cost no more than a focus group study, and considerably less than survey research with a large national sample.

Do obsess about getting the details exactly right in your experimental design. The test groups have to be made as equivalent as possible, and the test stimuli have to differ in precisely those respects, and only those respects, under investigation.

Don't be afraid to be a pioneer. Experimentation is one of several areas of market research where business-to-business and technology firms tend to lag far behind consumer goods firms as far as best practice is concerned.

Don't expect brilliant new ideas or stunning insights to emerge from experiments. Experimentation does one narrow thing extremely well: it reduces uncertainty about whether a specific message, price change, or product design is superior to another, or surmounts a specified hurdle rate. Experimentation is confirmatory market research par excellence; it is not a discovery tool.

References and Suggested Readings

Almquist, Eric, and Gordon Wyner. 2001. *Boost Your Marketing ROI with Experimental Design.* HBS #R0109K. Cambridge, MA: HBS Publishing.

A nice illustration of how procedures associated with conjoint studies can be applied in the context of a field experiment.

Dolan, Robert J. 1992. *Concept Testing.* HBS #9-590-063. Cambridge, MA: HBS Publishing.

Discusses the major approaches used to test new product concepts.

Lodish, Leonard, et al. 1995. How TV advertising works: A metaanalysis of 389 real world split cable T.V. advertising experiments. *Journal of Marketing Research* 32 (May): 125–139.

A fascinating examination of general principles revealed by split cable advertising experiments. Citations provide a guide to other studies in this vein.

Maples, Michael J., and Rolf M. Wolfsberg. 1987. The bottom line: Does industrial advertising sell? *Journal of Advertising Research* 27 (August/ September): RC 4–16.

Describes a field experiment using magazine ads in business-to-business markets.

McQuarrie, Edward F. 1998. Have laboratory experiments become detached from advertiser goals? *Journal of Advertising Research* 38: 15–26.

McQuarrie, Edward F. 2003. Integration of construct and external validity by means of proximal similarity: Implications for laboratory experiments in marketing. *Journal of Business Research* 57: 142–153.

I wrote these two papers to outline criteria for determining when a laboratory experiment can be generalized to real-world marketing contexts. The first article is accessible to practitioners, whereas the second is aimed at instructors who want a supplement to the well-known articles on this topic by Calder et al. and Lynch.

Sawyer, Alan G., Parker M. Worthing, and Paul E. Sendak. 1979. The role of laboratory experiments to test marketing strategies. *Journal of Marketing* 43 (Summer): 60–67.

Good introduction, using an extended example, to issues involved in using laboratory experiments to test marketing strategies.

Shocker, Allan D., and William G. Hall. 1986. Pretest market models: A critical evaluation. *Journal of Product Innovation Management* 3 (March): 86–107.

Discusses how the data from experiments can be transformed in order to produce reliable forecasts of market share; evaluates the strengths and weaknesses of various approaches to this problem.

11

Data Analysis

On the one hand, data analysis is a core competence of market research professionals. Thus, the Churchill and Iacobucci (2001) text devotes over 300 of its nearly 1,000 pages to this topic. On the other hand, the material in those chapters is virtually indistinguishable from what might be found in any text on applied statistics or statistics for the social sciences. In that sense, there is little that is unique about the data analyses performed for market research. In essence, the same statistical procedures are used across all the social sciences, and many of the practitioners of data analysis in market research have a Ph.D. in psychology, sociology, or economics. In fact, three specific statistical procedures, widely used in the social sciences, account for the bulk of the data analyses performed in day-to-day commercial market research. The limited goal of this chapter is to give the general manager and the engineering manager a handle on these procedures so that you know what to expect.

Given the brevity of this chapter, its goals must be especially limited. Think of it as a briefing. I can't teach you how to do data analysis in this space: that requires at least the hundreds of pages found in the standard market research text, or more properly the years of practice designing and conducting statistical analyses that form the core of most contemporary social science Ph.D. programs. What I can do is give you the names of things and put these names in a context. If this reduces your bewilderment, or increases your composure the next time a market research study is discussed, then you should be able to ask more critical questions, and ensure that the proposed study meets your needs as a decision maker. In addition, I hope to make you a more critical reader of secondary research and completed market research reports.

Procedure

First, an overview of how "data" come into existence and get analyzed and reported.

1. In most cases, somehow, some way, an Excel spreadsheet containing numbers corresponding to respondents' answers gets created. If the procedure was a Web-based survey, or involved computer-assisted telephone interviewing, or was administered on a computer (as in the case of many conjoint studies), then the Excel spreadsheet is created automatically as part of data collection. If paper forms were used, then someone entered the responses, represented numerically, into Excel. The Excel data are generally in matrix form ("flat file," in computerese) where the rows correspond to individual respondents and the columns contain each respondent's answers to each of the questions administered.

2. From Excel the data are typically imported to a specialized statistical analysis program. SPSS (www.spss.com) and SAS (www.sas.com) are two comprehensive packages used by many academics; numerous other such packages exist. Within the statistical package, raw data can be recorded, transformed, aggregated, or disaggregated at will, and virtually any statistical analysis can be performed by pulling down a menu and selecting a few options.

3. The data analyst is often a Ph.D., but routinized analyses on standardized instruments, such as a satisfaction questionnaire, may be performed by MBAs or other people who have accumulated hands-on experience. If the data originated in paper form, they have to be extensively checked for errors; even automatically generated data may be checked for logical consistency and for problematic respondents. If the study is a one-off affair, then the analyst will probably generate a variety of tentative analyses never seen by the client as the analyst assimilates the data and decides on a reporting approach. If the study is more routinized, then analysis may be as simple as pushing a button to trigger a canned series of tests. In this case, the analyst sees roughly the same output as the client.

4. The results of the analyses are formatted as tables and embedded into a narrative (which, in routinized cases, may be largely boilerplate).

5. Results are presented to the client and discussed. Depending on the contract and what was paid for, the research firm may attempt to add

quite a bit of interpretation to the data, to the point of recommending specific courses of action based on the data. Alternatively, the research firm may confine itself to explaining, clarifying, and defending the validity of the results and the procedures used, leaving substantive interpretation to client management.

Types of Data Analysis in Market Research

Most data analysis in market research consists of the following:

1. Tabulating and cross-tabulating proportions; an example would be agreement with an opinion item, cross-tabulated with brand owned.

2. Comparing means (averages) across items, groups of customers, or time periods; an example would be total annual expenditure on the product category for males versus females.

3. Predicting an outcome as a function of antecedent variables, as when level of satisfaction is shown to vary with expenditure, length of relationship with the vendor, number of changes in account team personnel, size of customer, and type of service contract.

Many more esoteric kinds of analyses, such as multidimensional scaling, also play a role in market research, but these three categories are the workhorses employed every day. In the case of each of these procedures, individual numbers are compared in an attempt to detect meaningful, or real, differences. How do customers of brand A differ from customers of brand B? Which attributes are worth a lot of money to customers, and which attributes are not worth any money? Which factors serve to increase customer satisfaction, and which have no effect?

Sometimes the reality of the difference between two numbers is deemed to be obvious, as in the following cross-tabulation:

	Brand A	Brand B
Agree	80%	20%
Disagree	20%	80%

If the sample is large, further statistical analysis of this comparison only confirms what we see at a glance—owners of different brands hold very different opinions. On the other hand, much of the time the data looks more like this:

Income	Brand A	Brand B	Brand C
<50,000	15%	12%	10%
50,000–100,000	30	31	28
100,000–250,000	47	43	49
>250,000	8	14	13

Or maybe like this:

Perceived Importance (10 = max)	Segment 1	Segment 2	Segment 3
Feature 1	8.6	7.6	8.3
Feature 2	7.0	8.2	8.8
Feature 3	6.2	7.5	7.9
Feature 4	5.9	4.0	5.8
Feature 5	3.8	5.6	5.7

As we move from 2×2 cross-tabulations to 3×5 cross-tabulations, and as the different results move closer and as the numbers become more abstract, as in the preference ratings, it becomes more and more difficult to say, with confidence, that customers of brand A have lower incomes than customers of brand B, or that different segments place different importance weights on key features.

If you recall the sampling chapter, you know that all these numbers obtained on the sample are only fallible estimates of the true population values in any case. The question becomes, When does a difference between two numbers in a report represent a reliable, actionable difference, and when is the difference only apparent, and dismissible as an artifact of the random variation inherent in all sample data? (Sometimes the question is more naturally thought of as whether two items have a real *association*; but this reduces to the question of whether the degree of association is different from zero. Hence, I shall refer to "difference" throughout this discussion.)

Modern statistical data analysis arose to address precisely this question: Which apparent differences in data are real and which are not? It is important to understand that statistical analysis gives us no direct access to the truth; it simply indicates whether the apparent difference is probably real, or alternatively, how probable it is that the apparent difference in the sample reflects a real difference in the population.

By convention, an apparent difference is accepted as a real difference if, when the appropriate test statistic is applied, it indicates that the difference in question would arise by chance in fewer than five of 100 cases. Now, let us unpack that unwieldy sentence. Every kind of data difference has associated with it one or more statistical procedures, and each such statistical procedure allows a computation of a number known as a test statistic. These test statistics are computed using the same sorts of assumptions about probability and probability distributions as underlay the discussion of sample size.

Suffice to say that when you calculate a test statistic, you acknowledge that if the study were repeated with a new probability sample, you would not get exactly the same results each time. This variability follows from the fact that we are drawing a limited sample from a very large population. The mathematics underlying the test statistic then envisions repeating the study an infinite number of times, and uses the data in the present sample to estimate how often, in that infinite series of repetitions, we would get a difference this big *by chance alone.* If the answer is fewer than five in 100, such results are generally given an asterisk and a footnote that reads something like "$p < .05$."

The important thing to retain from this discussion is that statistical analysis is simply a set of mathematically justified conventions for determining when we can accept an apparent difference as a real difference. More pointedly, if no statistical analysis has been applied, and the difference is not of the order 80–20 versus 20–80, you ought not to assume that the apparent difference is a real one. If you are reading a report that makes much of certain apparent differences—say, the 52% agreement in segment 1 versus the 43% agreement in segment 2—but that reports no statistical analysis, then you should become very suspicious. Worse, if there is a plethora of such statistical analyses, but the sample is not a probability sample, then you should question how much weight can be placed on the results; strictly speaking, in the absence of a probability sample, the results of the significance tests may be meaningless.

Managerial Perspective on Data Analysis

As a general manager receiving the results of data analyses, your primary responsibility is to understand that apparent differences need not be real differences. It behooves a general manager to have a deep humility concerning the ability of any research endeavor to produce a picture of the world as it truly is. Given this stance, you know to be skeptical as soon as you are intrigued. That is, when you see a difference that seems actionable or would resolve an uncertainty, your next response should always be, Is it real? Your second responsibility, then, is to understand the role played by statistical analysis in vetting apparent differences. You must have the discipline not to accept reported differences at face value, absent an appropriate test. Your final responsibility is to accept that even statistical analysis only provides an estimate of the odds that a difference is real rather than apparent. It takes quite a bit of tough-mindedness to accept that some proportion of statistical judgments indicating that a difference is real will be wrong—about five in 100, actually. Because general managers may encounter hundreds of data comparisons in a year, they can be virtually certain that some differences vetted as real are not. As I said at the outset, market research reduces uncertainty but cannot eliminate it.

Put in more positive terms, if a good sample was drawn (a correctly sized probability sample), and if two key numbers appear to be really different $(p < .05)$, and you have no countervailing data or experience, then you should feel comfortable acting on these results. More than 95 times out of 100 the data will be vindicated. But remember: it is never 100% certain.

Reference and Suggested Readings

Churchill, Gilbert A., and Dawn Iacobucci. 2001. *Marketing Research: Methodological Foundations,* 8th ed. Chicago: Southwestern.

> You can consult standard market research texts to get an overview of the statistical techniques used to analyze market research data. If a particular kind of analysis is of interest, Sage Publications offers hundreds of books devoted to specific data analysis procedures, and their Web site can be searched using the name of the technique.

PART III

12

Combining Research Techniques into Research Strategies

I t is rarely the case that a business problem can be addressed by the application of a single research technique in isolation. More commonly multiple complementary research techniques, conducted in sequence, are required. This chapter describes the kind of complete research strategy that might be developed to address five common business problems. The examples given are "pure" cases, showing what you might do when the magnitude of the problem justifies it and your budget permits it. In actual cases, one or more of the techniques described might be omitted, for the very good reason that the payback for the research expenditure would be too small, in accordance with the calculations described in the appendix to Chapter 2. Other combinations of techniques could also be used; these sequences are intended to be illustrative and not rigid prescriptions.

Developing New Products

- Use *secondary research* to assess existing product offerings from competitors and to estimate market size and growth rates in this category. Secondary data can also be used to build a financial justification for any proposed product.

- Conduct *customer visits* among potential buyers for the new product. These visits identify unmet needs and areas of dissatisfaction with existing offerings. Participation in the visits by engineering staff will assist them throughout the project in visualizing how customers might respond to various design trade-offs.

• Execute a *conjoint analysis* study to identify the optimal combination of features and functionality from among several design alternatives produced in response to the secondary research and customer visits.

• Conduct an *experiment* to estimate profitability and market share for the new product at each of several prices.

Assessing Customer Satisfaction

• Use *secondary research* to find any public information on competitors' level of customer satisfaction, plus any data on one's own level of customer satisfaction that outsiders might have gathered. In addition to these quantitative data, search the literature for more qualitative data: what are the key dissatisfiers or common complaints? What are crucial needs that must be addressed by any satisfactory solution? Analyze your own internal records to identify themes running through complaints, calls to the service department, and the like.

• Conduct *customer visits* to identify and explore how customers evaluate their satisfaction with this product category, what standards they use to assess product quality, and how intangibles such as vendor reputation come into play. The goal here is to learn *what* to measure.

• Conduct a *survey* of customers at regular intervals to numerically measure and track customer satisfaction. This survey needs to draw a representative sample and it needs to be executed consistently over time. Here you precisely and accurately measure the factors you earlier identified and explored via secondary research and customer visits.

• Follow up on surprising, unexpected, or confusing results with a program of *customer visits*. Although surveys tell *that* something is wrong, they don't always explain *why* customers are less satisfied or what needs to be done to improve.

Segmenting a Market

• Use *secondary research* to identify possible segmentation schemes proposed by industry analysts or actually in use by competitors. Pay close attention to internal secondary data in the form of sales records and customer databases. Exploratory analyses of these internal data may suggest significant differences among existing customers.

- Use *focus groups* to explore psychological differences among customers. These might concern values, or benefits desired, or intangible cultural or lifestyle differences. Focus groups are helpful in this application because participants often polarize around discussion of certain issues, thus highlighting possible segment differences. The goal here is to discover new ways to segment the market.

- Conduct *customer visits* to explore in depth the characteristics of the possible segments identified through secondary research and focus groups. The visits assist in developing a detailed profile of each segment, and may also suggest new segments or new ways to reconfigure the tentative segmentation scheme.

- Conduct a *survey* to accurately measure the size and characteristics of each segment in the tentative scheme. Although your earlier research has generated possible segments, it cannot confirm that any particular segment is large enough to be worthwhile, nor whether the tentative segments actually differ in the marketplace to the degree suggested by your research studies. Because segmentation analyses are typically a prelude to a decision to target one or a small number of segments, it is important to do survey research to accurately assess how attractive each individual segment might be.

- Conduct a *choice modeling* study to understand how brand perceptions and product preferences differ across segments of interest. Given two or more targeted segments whose attractiveness has been demonstrated through survey research, the question now becomes how to develop differentiated messages and actual products that precisely address the distinctive wants and needs of each targeted segment. The choice modeling study can show how perceptions of your brand differ across segments, thus providing a focus for future advertising efforts, and also how importance weights differ, thus directing product development efforts.

Expanding Into New Markets

Here the notion is that you might be able to sell current or modified products to new types of customers.

- Use *secondary research* to identify attractive markets not currently served. A comparison of industry data to your own sales records and customer databases helps to identify underserved or neglected markets. Profiles of competitors might reveal to you unsuspected market niches, or areas where, despite good sales volume, you have barely penetrated.

- Conduct *focus groups* to gain initial insights into the thought world and point of view of members of untapped markets. Focus groups tend to be a time-efficient means of grasping the basic outline of an unfamiliar worldview.

- Conduct *customer visits* to more thoroughly describe applications, usage environments, and organizational decision processes of these untapped markets. The observational component and the in-depth nature of the interaction makes visits a useful supplement to focus groups.

- Conduct a *survey* to more thoroughly describe the size characteristics and potential of the one or more new markets under study. (Note that the same logic applies to markets as to segments within markets.)

- Conduct a *conjoint analysis* study to grasp what is important and unimportant to these people so as to develop or select the best product configuration with which to attack this new market.

Developing an Advertising Campaign

- Use *secondary research* to identify competitors' level of spending, relative emphasis on various media, and choice of particular vehicles. Gather as well examples of competitors' actual ads so as to identify themes and appeals.

- Conduct *focus groups* to gain insight into customers' thinking and to understand the kinds of issues that are important and unimportant to them. It will be important to have both vendor marketing staff and advertising agency personnel be involved with these focus groups.

- Conduct a *survey* to describe brand image of self and competitors, current levels of awareness, and specific beliefs or perceptions about your brand. The goal here is partly to verify findings from the focus groups, and partly to measure baseline levels of factors, such as awareness, that the advertising campaign is supposed to influence.

• Conduct an *experiment* to compare the relative effectiveness of several alternative executions, each of which is on strategy, in the sense of addressing issues uncovered in the earlier research, but each of which takes a somewhat different creative approach. Sometimes the goal here will be to pick the strongest execution, and at other times it will be to rank order the effectiveness of a larger group so that the more effective executions receive a larger media budget.

• Conduct a *survey* to track the effectiveness of the campaign. This survey repeats measurements made during the baseline survey.

Commentary

The common theme across most of these research strategies should be apparent. The canonical sequence of techniques in devising a research strategy is as follows: first, secondary research; second, customer visits or focus groups for exploratory purposes; and third, surveys or conjoint analysis or experiments, for confirmatory purposes. Again, your specific application may differ, so that other sequences or more extended sequences may also be valid. Moreover, much depends on the unique circumstances of your case as to whether a particular technique needs to be executed at all. But the canonical sequence, stated more generally, serves as a useful summary for the marketing research advice given in this book:

First, look around.

Second, explore in depth.

Third, identify the best option.

Fourth, measure the results of your decision.

Index

About the Author

Edward F. McQuarrie is a professor in the Department of Marketing, Leavey School of Business, Santa Clara University. He received his Ph.D. in social psychology from the University of Cincinnati in 1985.

His research interests include customer value, qualitative research, and market research appropriate to technology products, on the one hand, and advertising research, rhetoric, and semiotics on the other. He has also written the book *Customer Visits: Building a Better Market Focus,* and published articles in the *Journal of Consumer Research, Journal of Consumer Psychology, Journal of Product Innovation Management, Marketing Management, Marketing Research, Journal of the Market Research Society, Journal of Advertising Research,* and the *Journal of Advertising.* He serves on the editorial board of the *Journal of Consumer Research.*

He is currently Associate Dean for Assessment and Improvement at the Leavey School of Business, responsible for the assessment of learning outcomes and the evaluation of teaching. He was Associate Dean for Graduate Studies, 1996–2000, responsible for the MBA and Executive MBA programs.

Professor McQuarrie has moderated focus groups since 1980 for Burke Marketing Research, among others. He has consulted for a variety of technology firms, and has taught seminars on effective customer visits, managing focus group research, marketing research methods, and similar topics for Hewlett-Packard, Sun Microsystems, Microsoft, Apple Computer, Tektronix, Varian Associates, Cadence Design, and other clients.